Rockhounding New Mexico

Help Us Keep This Guide Up to Date

Every effort has been made by the authors and editors to make this guide as accurate and useful as possible. However, many things can change after a guide is published— trails are rerouted, regulations change, techniques evolve, facilities come under new management, and so forth.

We welcome your comments concerning your experiences with this guide and how you feel it could be improved and kept up to date. While we may not be able to respond to all comments and suggestions, we'll take them to heart and we'll also make certain to share them with the authors. Please send your comments and suggestions to the following address:

The Globe Pequot Press
Reader Response/Editorial Department
P.O. Box 480
Guilford, CT 06437

Or you may e-mail us at:

editorial@GlobePequot.com

Thanks for your input, and happy rockhounding!

Rockhounding New Mexico

A Guide to 140 of the State's Best Rockhounding Sites

Ruta Vaskys and Martin Freed

FALCONGUIDES ®

GUILFORD, CONNECTICUT
HELENA MONTANA

FALCONGUIDES®

Copyright © 2008 by Rowman & Littlefield

Falcon and FalconGuides are registered trademarks of Rowman & Littlefield.

Excerpt in Site 111, by Merrill O. Murphy, originally appeared in the *Newsletter of the New Mexico Faceters Guild*. Used by permission of the New Mexico Faceters Guild.
Photos by Martin Freed and Ruta Vaskys unless noted otherwise.
Maps created by Scott Lockheed © Rowman & Littlefield

Library of Congress Cataloging-in-Publication Data

Vaskys, Ruta.
  Rockhounding New Mexico : a guide to 140 of the state's best rockhounding sites / Ruta Vaskys and Martin Freed.
    p. cm.
  ISBN 978-0-7627-4376-6
  1. Rocks—Collection and preservation—New Mexico—Guidebooks. 2. New Mexico—Guide-books. I. Freed, Martin. II. Title.

QE445.N6.F74 2008
552.09789—dc22

2008024631

Printed in the United States of America

Distributed by NATIONAL BOOK NETWORK

To Martin's mother, Evelyn Freed, who was responsible for igniting our passion for rockhounding. She spent most of her life scouring the mountains of the Southwest searching for that fist-sized diamond. We're sure she is still looking.

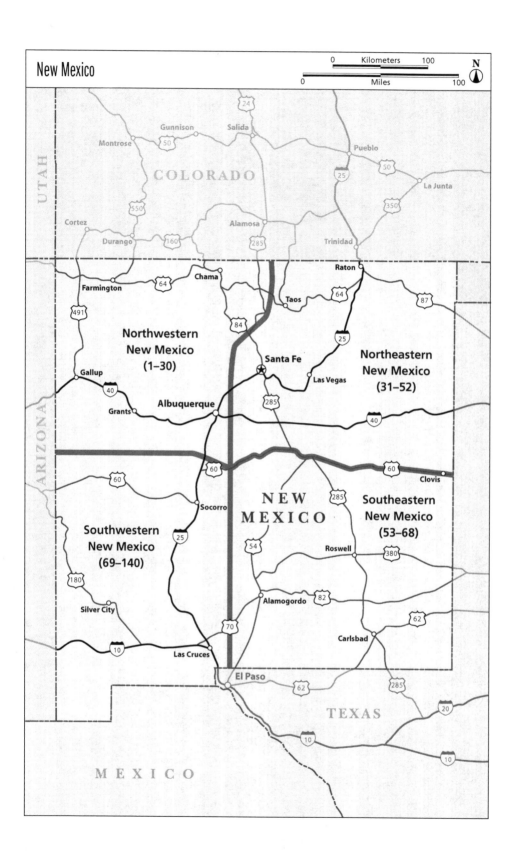

Contents

NORTHEASTERN NEW MEXICO

SOUTHEASTERN NEW MEXICO

SOUTHWESTERN NEW MEXICO

Acknowledgments

We would like to thank all the dedicated public servants of the Bureau of Land Management and the USDA Forest Service. These folks diligently work to keep our federal public lands open and safe. They are also very helpful if you are trying to find a particular old mine or agate area.

Introduction

We were about a third of the way through the research for this book when we decided to take a break for a day and sit in the hot pools at Gila Hot Springs north of Silver City. The dip was shared by a number of folks, including an attractive young woman who was explaining to the rest of us how all of the wonderful rocks in New Mexico were formed by the convergence of a number of vortexes. "More vortexes come together over the Land of Enchantment than anywhere else in the world," she declared.

We must admit that it is an interesting theory, but whether this is the case or if it is just plain old geology, rockhounding in New Mexico is outstanding. Whether your primary interest is finding cutting material like agates or chrysocolla or sifting the sand for marine fossils indicative of ages past, New Mexico is indeed the Land of Enchantment for prospectors of all degrees of skill and persistence.

Between the two of us, we have almost sixty years of prospecting under our belts. We have scoured the landscape from Newfoundland to Alaska to Florida to southern Mexico and everywhere in between. Over the years, guidebooks have been a valuable tool; however, they have had their shortcomings. Often they are out of date. The author might have been to the location thirty years ago, and when the reader shows up at the site, he or she may find a subdivision on top of the agate bed. In addition, roads change, as do landmarks. Some guides indicate that they've been revised, but often the changes are just the addition of a few sites, while it is apparent that the author had not revisited the locations.

Another gripe that we have with some guidebooks is that they often build up the reader's expectations. They give a list of minerals that may be found, but many are rather scarce. We attempt to give the reader a realistic idea of what they may be able to find at each site by noting in the rockhounding description whether we found the materials ourselves or whether they have been reported by others. We often also state how much time we spent at a location and exactly how many pieces of each mineral we found.

Over the years we often complained about guidebooks. In fact, we griped so much that our rockhounding friends said, "Why don't you write your own book?" So here we are.

How to Use This Book

During the two months preceding the writing of this guidebook, we visited over 110 of the 140 sites included herein. Of the remaining thirty, ten were personally prospected during the past few years. Information about the remaining twenty came from friends, rockhounds, and other sources. When this was the case, we indicated so in those sites' descriptions.

While it is not necessary to have a Global Positioning System (GPS) to find any of the areas described in this book, we give latitude and longitude readings for most of the sites. We also indicate where the readings were taken—on top of the tailings pile, at the beginning of the road into the mine, etc.—when this information was useful. When using other guidebooks, we found it frustrating not knowing whether we actually found the site described. The GPS coordinates can confirm that the reader did indeed find the correct location.

For the purpose of this book, we divide New Mexico into four sections: Northwestern, Northeastern, Southeastern, and Southwestern. The east–west division is a line starting at the southern part of the state separating Dona Ana County to the west and Otero to the east, continuing north between Socorro County to the west and Lincoln to the east, and finally reaching the Rio Grande, where the line follows the river to the northern border of the state. All sites to the west of this line are either in the Northwestern or Southwestern sections. The north–south separator begins at the Arizona border and follows the line between Cibola and Catron Counties until it reaches Interstate 25, from which it follows U.S. Highway 60 to the Texas border. All sites to the north of this line are either in the Northwestern or Northeastern sections.

Within each section, the sites are more-or-less numbered east to west, then north to south. This is not always the case, however, when a bunch of sites are clustered in a small geographic area. In those instances, we tried to number the agglomerated collecting areas consecutively.

Hazards and Precautions

Snakes

Although snakebite incidents are relatively rare when compared to the number of people roaming around New Mexico, anyone venturing into the wilderness should take certain precautions. Not all snakebites can be prevented, but a few simple steps will greatly reduce the risk:

- Know how to identify poisonous and nonvenomous species.
- Take a snakebite kit and become familiar with its use.
- Know where to go for help.
- Know the most common symptoms of snakebite:
  - bloody discharge at wound site
  - fang marks
  - swelling at the site of the bite
  - severe localized pain and discoloration
  - swollen lymph nodes near bite
  - diarrhea, burning, convulsions, fainting, and/or dizziness

The symptoms may resemble other medical conditions. Consult a physician if you think you've been bitten.

Treatment for snakebites: *Stay calm and act quickly.* Get help fast, but while waiting for assistance, do the following:

- Wash the bite with soap and water.
- Keep the bitten area lower than the heart.
- Apply a cool compress.
- Monitor breathing and heart rate.
- Remove all rings, watches, and constrictive clothing, in case of swelling.

If unable to get help within thirty minutes, the American Red Cross recommends the following:

- Apply a bandage, wrapped 2 to 4 inches above the bite, to help slow the venom. This should not cut off the flow of blood from a vein or artery—the band should be loose enough to slip a finger under it.
- A suction device can be placed over the bite to help draw venom out of the wound without making cuts. These devices are often included in commercial snakebite kits.

Prevention: Of course, it's best to prevent a snakebite to begin with. Take the following precautions:

- Do not harass any snake (or any other wildlife for that matter). Many bites occur as a result of someone trying to kill a snake or get too close to it.
- Do not walk through tall grass unless absolutely necessary. Stick to the hiking paths as much as possible.

- Watch where you put your hands and feet.
- Be especially cautious when rock climbing.

Most important, do not let a fear of snakes stop you from having a good time in the outdoors. Bites are very rare—just take some precautions.

Insects and Arachnids

The following critters are more annoying than snakes—and can be just as dangerous. Just a few simple precautions, however, can save the day.

Mosquitoes: These are the most common pests. In some areas of the state, especially the lowlands, they could carry diseases, some of which are life-threatening. However, they can be easily deterred by taking the following steps:

- Use a repellent. Many experts believe that the most effective are products that contain DEET. The higher the percentage of this ingredient, the better. If you do not want to use DEET, Natrapel works but perhaps not as well.
- Mosquitoes are most active around dusk. Staying indoors during this time will limit exposure.
- Cover as much of your skin as possible with clothing. Some people also wear head nets.

No-see-ums, or gnats: If you ever have to spend a night dealing with these guys, it will be long remembered. Some call them sand fleas, as they are usually found in sandy or gravelly areas. They are small enough to pass through all but the finest screens, so make sure your tent or camper is so outfitted.

DEET works well on no-see-ums, and we have spread it on our screens with some success. Since these insects are attracted to light, it is best to do your reading before dark.

Ticks: Various species of ticks are found throughout New Mexico. A bite from an infected tick can result in a serious disease. Here are a few precautions:

- These guys hang on foliage, waiting for a host to walk by. Stay on rocky or sandy trails.
- Rub insect repellent on your legs.
- Wear your pants inside your socks and put repellent on them. White socks are best because the ticks will be easier to spot.
- Check your skin for ticks every evening, or have your partner do it for you.

- If you happen to get a tick bite, keep in mind that the longer the critter is attached, the more likely it is to pass a disease on to you. If you cannot get professional medical help quickly, take a good pair of tweezers, grab your skin below the tick's mouth, and pull it off. Dab with alcohol and bandage.

Spiders: A few poisonous spiders inhabit New Mexico, but very few spider bites are reported. Folks usually get stung when they roll over onto the critter or try to scratch it as it is walking up their body. Stay aware of what is going on around you.

Scorpions: Many species of scorpions inhabit New Mexico, but only one is dangerous to humans: *Centruroides exilicauda*. While found in good numbers in Arizona, they are quite scarce in the Land of Enchantment. In the few areas where they do show up, however, they can be abundant. The best way to protect yourself is look at the bottom of every rock you pick up. Drop it immediately if a scorpion is present. Also, if you take off your boots, check them for scorpions and spiders before putting them back on.

Bears

Black bears are common in the mountainous forests of New Mexico. These guys are very shy, and you should consider yourself lucky if you see one. However, a few precautions should be taken not so much to protect humans from bears, but the other way around. It's usually the carelessness of humans that produces a nuisance animal, and occasionally one has to be dispatched.

- Always keep your food in bear-proof containers.
- Keep your campsite clean and neat.
- Do not throw garbage into open receptacles. We've noticed that some areas in the western part of the state now have bear-proof garbage cans.
- Head in the opposite direction, very slowly, if you see a cub.

Cougars

While these large cats are generally scarce in New Mexico, they can be relatively abundant in certain areas. If you are in higher-elevation forest, which could be mountain lion country, keep a close eye on children and pets. If attacked, act aggressively: pick up a big stick, throw rocks at it (not the agates you just picked up), etc. The cat will almost always be intimidated and go find easier prey.

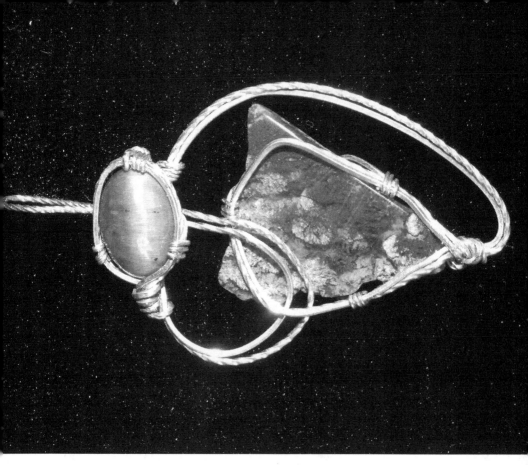

A pendant made from Chavez Canyon agate.

Other Mammals

While raccoons, possums, foxes, coyotes, jackrabbits, and other small mammals are not usually a threat, rabies could be a problem. This disease can make even the shyest critters aggressive. If you see any animal acting strangely, do not approach it. Move away.

Poison Ivy and Poison Oak

Most people are at least somewhat allergic to the oils produced by these two plants. The best way to protect yourself is to learn to identify them and make sure you are not exposed. Standard clothing does not help very much, since the oil can penetrate the fabric and reach your skin. In fact, you can develop the symptoms by touching the affected clothes after they are taken off. The oils can also be spread from person to person by touching.

In order not to ruin a trip, take an antihistamine salve along just in case someone develops the rash. A number of good ones can be bought over the counter at most pharmacies. If the condition is severe, seek medical help.

The Sun

The sun is very strong in New Mexico. If you are fair-skinned, be sure to include a good sunscreen in your supplies. It should have an SPF of at least 25. The best way to treat sunburn is to avoid it. However, if it happens, a number of over-the-counter remedies are available that can treat the discomfort and minimize the chance of infection.

Mild cases of sunburn can be treated by taking a cool shower or applying cold cloth compresses. The application of topical agents such as aloe vera and/or salves containing hydrocortisone could be helpful. Severe sunburn should be treated by a medical professional. Do not wait until you get home— find a local doctor or even an emergency room if necessary.

The symptoms of sun poisoning are fever, nausea, vomiting, fatigue, dizziness, red skin rash, and/or chills. Seek medical help at once.

Boating

Occasionally people use boats to reach good rockhounding sites in New Mexico. Be aware of the boating regulations and what equipment is needed. Each vessel should be equipped with one personal flotation device (PFD) for each individual on board, in the appropriate sizes for kids and adults. Some boats require fire extinguishers, whistles, flares, and running lights. These things do get checked.

Know Your Limits

Some of the sites require rigorous hiking. If the hike starts off downhill, remember that while it might be easy heading in, you will have a more strenuous hike back up, especially carrying all those rocks you found. Do not wear yourself out beyond your ability to get back to the parking lot.

Abandoned Mines

Be extra careful around abandoned mines. Vertical shafts may be overgrown with vegetation and not readily apparent.

Do not go into any mine shaft unless you know what you are doing and have backup help. Most old mines have lots of boards and trash lying around. Look out for rusty nails and other sharp things protruding from wood. You can also get badly cut by stuff like old metal, glass, or even tailings. Be careful.

Back Road Driving

If you pursue this avocation, sooner or later you will find yourself on a really terrible road heading uphill with a vertical drop-off on one side. Sure enough, you will meet a vehicle coming down the road and there are no pull-offs. What do you do? Remember that the vehicle going uphill has the right-of-way, as it is much more dangerous backing down than up. While driving down these one-lane roads, try to remember where the turnouts are so you will know how far you would have to back up if need be.

Some of these roads are rather steep. If you drive a big truck like us, when you reach a crest, you often cannot see the road over the hood. Do not assume that the tracks are straight ahead—the road could make a sharp turn. Either step out yourself or have a passenger get out to see where the path heads.

If the road ahead looks bad, do not continue driving. Get out and take a look. Remember that four-wheel drive is there to get you out of trouble, not into trouble.

The Weather

Everyone knows that the Southwestern desert gets very hot in the summer. If you are 10 miles into the backcountry and your vehicle breaks down, you'd better have enough water to hike out. Better yet, be sure your vehicle is in good shape before heading into the area. Also make sure you have enough fuel.

Certain parts of New Mexico can be very cold in the winter. Be prepared if you are heading into the mountains. The road could be cut off by a big snowstorm, so carry extra blankets or sleeping bags and food and water for such an occurrence.

Rainstorms are also dangerous, especially at high elevations. Lightning strikes can kill. If the weather is threatening, do not throw on your backpack and start up the trail. During wet periods, many roads become impassable. Make sure the road is OK before heading out, or better yet, wait for dry weather.

Where You Are Allowed to Collect

A large portion of the land in New Mexico is federally owned and open to the public. The Bureau of Land Management (BLM) controls much of it and allows collecting on its property with certain restrictions. Rockhounds must not create a significant disturbance. You can dig, but not to the point where it can cause additional erosion. In other words, fill in your holes before leaving. It is also requested that you not drive onto soft soil because the tracks can increase erosion.

The BLM allows the collection of small amounts of minerals for personal use. "Small" is not specifically defined. We imagine that a bag or two would be OK, but a pickup load is not.

Petrified wood is more restricted. Rockhounds are allowed 25 pounds per day and not more than 250 pounds in a year. Invertebrate and plant fossils can be collected without restriction except in designated areas, but vertebrate (fish, reptile, mammal, and bird) artifacts cannot be collected on BLM land.

The regulations for the national forests are about the same, except there does not appear to be the 25-pound-per-day (250-pound-per-year) petrified wood limit. Small amounts of these minerals are allowed to be collected, but often the limits are not clearly spelled out. Check with the Forest Service for specific regulations. Fossil regulations are the same as those for BLM land.

Collecting is not permitted in national parks, national monuments, and wilderness areas. Native American lands are private and you must have permission to collect, which is rarely granted. You can often get permission from private landowners to collect on their property, but this takes time and effort. It is very important that you go through the process, however, and not trespass.

Rockhounding Ethics

Mineral collecting is a fascinating and enjoyable avocation. We rockhounds have a code of ethics that must be followed to enable us to continue to enjoy our passion. Here are the self-imposed restrictions that we abide by:

- Never collect more than you can use. Leave some for the next group of rockhounds.
- When you dig holes, always fill them in.
- Do not leave big tire ruts that could cause additional erosion.
- Always be sure that you are collecting on public land or have permission.
- Carry out any trash you produce, and if you see anybody else's consider picking that up too.
- Always leave gates as you found them. If they were open, leave them open. If they were closed, close them behind you.
- Be very careful when making campfires. The Southwest is generally very dry, making the brush extremely susceptible to fires. If you must build a campfire, make sure you do so in a well-made fire ring, and douse the fire completely afterward. Better yet, do your cooking on a small camp stove.

Legend

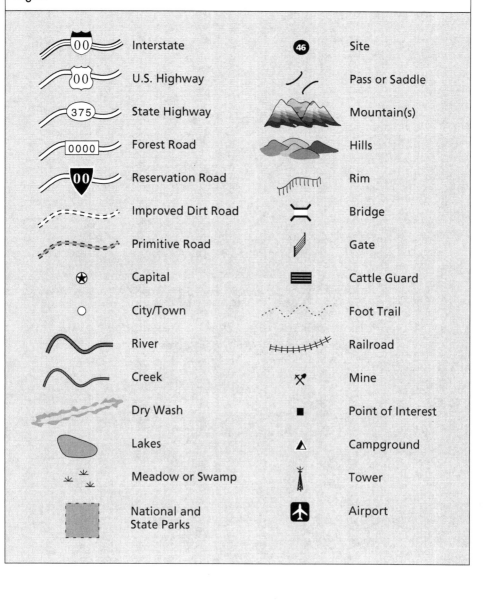

Interstate	Site
U.S. Highway	Pass or Saddle
State Highway	Mountain(s)
Forest Road	Hills
Reservation Road	Rim
Improved Dirt Road	Bridge
Primitive Road	Gate
Capital	Cattle Guard
City/Town	Foot Trail
River	Railroad
Creek	Mine
Dry Wash	Point of Interest
Lakes	Campground
Meadow or Swamp	Tower
National and State Parks	Airport

Northwestern New Mexico

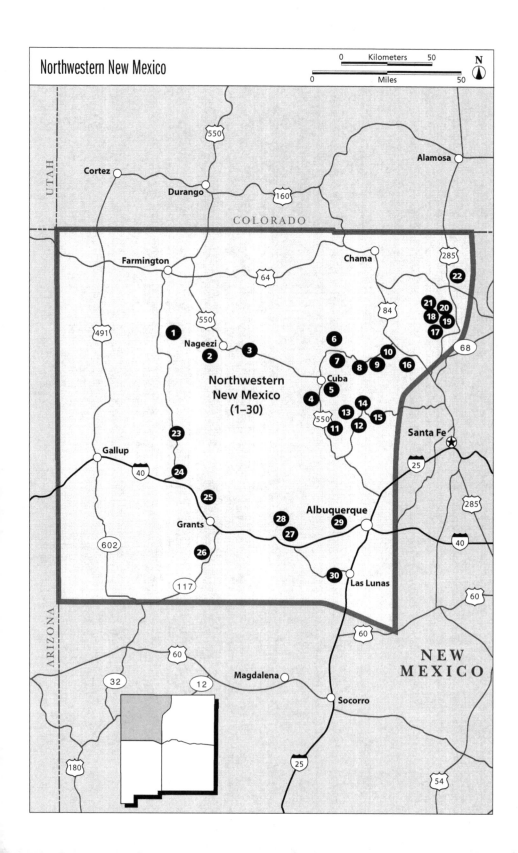

Northwestern New Mexico

Bisti Badlands

Land type: High desert.
Best time of year: All year.
Land manager: Bureau of Land Management, Farmington District.
Tools: None.
Vehicle: Any.
Precautions and restrictions: Wilderness area. No collecting allowed.
Special attractions: The Chaco Culture National Historical Park offers a look at the culture at the center of pueblo life between 850 and 1250 AD, in addition to camping, hiking, and a museum.
Finding the site: This wilderness area is located southeast of Farmington and northeast of Thoreau. From exit 53 off Interstate 40 in Thoreau, take Highway 371 north 70.1 miles. Turn right (east) on County Road 7297, which continues into the Bisti Wilderness to a dead end at 3.9 miles.

The Bisti Badlands are a must-see.

Rockhounding

The Bisti Badlands is full of unique geological formations. It is incredibly picturesque, with banded wavelike mounds. The layers are extremely colorful, from brown to white to rust to yellow to red and all the shades in between. The Bisti Wilderness Area covers 4,000 acres of high desert and is administered by the Bureau of Land Management (BLM). This is a must-see for anyone interested in geological processes, and besides, it is quite close to a few collecting areas.

Split Lip Flats

Land type: High desert.

GPS: N36° 12' 43" / W107° 58' 15".

Elevation: 6,347 feet.

Best time of year: March through November.

Land manager: New Mexico Department of Transportation.

Material: Agate, petrified wood, carnelian, jasper, and limb casts.

Tools: Geological hammer, small shovel, and spray bottle.

Vehicle: From Thoreau, any vehicle would be OK during dry weather, but from Blanco Trading Post, a four-wheel drive with high clearance is preferred.

Precautions and restrictions: This is a remote area. Carry enough water and fuel, and be sure your vehicle is in good working order. The roads can get quite muddy during wet periods. There is lots of private land in the area, so be sure not to trespass. It can be snaky during the warm months.

Special attractions: The Chaco Culture National Historical Park offers a look at the culture at the center of pueblo life between 850 and 1250 AD, in addition to camping, hiking, and a museum. Bisti Badlands is also nearby (see site 1).

Finding the site: This area is located east of the Bisti Badlands. From exit 53 off Interstate 40 in Thoreau, take Highway 371 north for 60.6 miles. Turn right (east) on gravel County Road 7650. A sign at the beginning of the road indicates that this is the way to Nageezi Chapter House. After 7.6 miles, County Road 7870 intersects from the south. Stay on CR 7650 and cross a cattle guard in another 0.1 mile (7.7 miles). Continue to mile 10.9, which brings you well into the collecting area. You can find material for at least another 5.4 miles.

From Blanco Trading Post, the route to the area is rather confusing. It is easy to get lost, so pay close attention to our directions. From the junction of U.S. Highway 550 and Highway 57, drive southwest on Highway 57, which is a gravel road for 10.5 miles. Turn right (west) onto CR 7650 and cross a cattle guard. This will bring you to the start of the collecting area, which goes on for at least 5.4 miles.

Rockhounding

A lot of material can be found in this area. Much of the land here is private, but enough can be picked up in the right-of-way to make this trip very worthwhile. The carnelian and jasper pieces are quite small but great for tumbling. The petrified wood is well agatized and nice cutting material. The agates range from banded to moss to clear and white. The limb casts are well formed and mostly of neutral color.

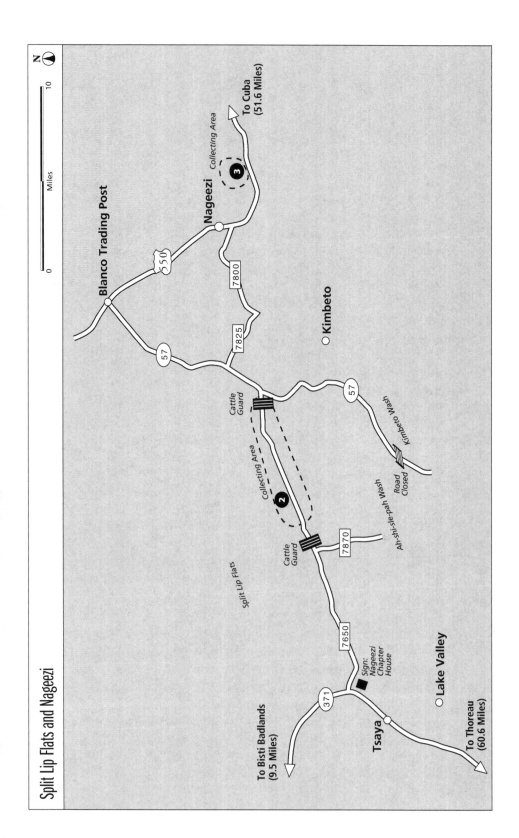

Split Lip Flats and Nageezi

Nageezi

See map on page 16.

Land type: High desert.

GPS: N36° 14' 53" / W107° 41' 28".

Elevation: 6,845 feet.

Best time of year: March through November.

Land manager: Bureau of Land Management, Farmington District.

Material: Petrified wood, agate, jasper, and barite.

Tools: Geological hammer, small shovel, and spray bottle.

Vehicle: Any vehicle will do unless you want to drive down to the wash, in which case a high-clearance four-wheel drive is necessary.

Precautions and restrictions: The dirt road is very rough. Make sure your vehicle can handle it before proceeding down from the top.

Special attractions: The Chaco Culture National Historical Park offers a look at the culture at the center of pueblo life between 850 and 1250 AD, in addition to camping, hiking, and a museum. Bisti Badlands is also nearby (see site 1).

Nageezi agate can be found throughout this area.

Finding the site: This area can be found just a little southeast of Nageezi. From Nageezi, drive southeast on U.S. Highway 550 for 3 miles to where County Road 7900 intersects on the right (south). Continue on US 550 for another mile, then turn left onto a dirt road leading east. Park as soon as you are able.

Rockhounding

A lot of fine tumbling material can be found here, along with a few larger pieces appropriate for cutting. You can start right where you park and then walk down and follow the wash for several miles. We located our best agates and petrified wood within 100 yards of the parking area. Here we also found some of the brightest pieces of red jasper. They are small and great for tumbling.

We did not find any barite, although it has been reported here in the form of balls. We only explored about a half mile down the road, but we're sure that with more time, there are lots of treasures to be found here.

Cuba Petrified Wood

Land type: High desert.
GPS: N35° 58' 24" / W107° 00' 23".
Elevation: 6,777 feet.
Best time of year: March through November.
Land manager: New Mexico Department of Transportation.
Material: Petrified wood, carnelian and other agates, and palm wood.
Tools: Geological hammer, small shovel, large shovel, sledgehammer, goggles, spray bottle, chisels, and gads.
Vehicle: Any vehicle will do to the tracks to the mesa, but a very rugged four-wheel drive is necessary if you intend to drive to the mesa.
Precautions and restrictions: The final road to the Mesa de Cuba is very rough.
Special attractions: A number of private and public hot springs are located near Jemez Springs, in addition to the Soda Dam (see site 12). Both attractions are relatively close when you can drive over the mountain on Highway 126, which is closed in winter.
Finding the site: This area is located southwest of Cuba under Mesa de Cuba. From the junction of U.S. Highway 550 and Highway 126 in Cuba, head south on US 550 for 0.9 mile. Turn right (west) onto Highway 197 and continue for 4.2 miles, then turn right (west) onto tracks leading toward the mesa, which is visible in the distance. The road is very rough, so we recommend that you park and then walk toward the mesa, which is about a mile away.

Rockhounding

Due to time restraints, we only hiked about a half mile toward the mesa and found just a few small pieces of petrified wood, carnelian, and other agates. Others have reported finding large pieces of wood, including some palm wood. Diligent hiking and searching closer to the mesa may produce better finds.

Cuba Minerals

Land type: Mountainous forest.
GPS: N35° 59' 43" / W106° 50' 35" (start of Forest Road 267).
Elevation: 8,762 feet.
Best time of year: June through September.
Land manager: Bureau of Land Management, Farmington District.
Material: Chalcocite, chalcopyrite, azurite, chrysalcola, and malachite.
Tools: Geological hammer, small shovel, sledgehammer, goggles, and spray bottle.
Vehicle: Any vehicle will do until Forest Road 267, but a rugged four-wheel drive is needed if you intend to attempt to drive the road.
Precautions and restrictions: Highway 126 is very windy and is icy for a big part of the year.
Special attractions: A number of private and public hot springs are located near Jemez Springs, in addition to the Soda Dam (see site 12). Both attractions are relatively close when you can drive over the mountain on Highway 126, which is closed in winter.
Finding the site: This site is located in the mountains southeast of Cuba. From the junction of U.S. Highway 550 and Highway 126 in Cuba, drive southeast on Highway 126 for 9.7 miles. FR 267 is on the left (north) side; you can park on the right (south). The road is relatively rough, but the mine is only a half mile in.

Rockhounding

We have attempted to get to this mine a few times, but it has always been snow-covered. We are, therefore, reporting what others related to us. Good luck, but wait until June to make the trip—and please leave a few pieces for us.

Gallina Agate

Land type: Mountainous forest.
GPS: N36° 14' 15" / W106° 51' 18" (beginning of final road).
Elevation: 7,340 feet.
Best time of year: April though October.
Land manager: Bureau of Land Management, Farmington District.
Material: Agate and jasper.
Tools: Geological hammer, large shovel, sledgehammer, large pick, chisels, goggles, and gads.
Vehicle: Any vehicle is OK when it's dry, but four-wheel drive is recommended during wet periods.
Precautions and restrictions: The road to the agate area can be very slippery when wet.
Special attractions: Abiquiu Reservoir boasts fine angling and scenery.
Finding the site: This agate area is located northeast of Cuba and northwest of the small town of Gallina. From the junction of U.S. Highway 550 and Highway 126 in Cuba, drive northwest on US 550 for 3.7 miles. Turn right (north) onto Highway 96 and continue for 12.9 miles to its junction with Highway 112, where Highway 96 makes a sharp turn to the right (east). Continue on Highway 96 for 4.1 miles. The unnamed road to the agate area is on the left (north).

Rockhounding

Though other guides report this area as being open, we found the road posted. The sign said that there is seasonal access, probably coinciding with the hunting seasons. Perhaps between September and January you can go and discover this area, which reportedly contains agate and jasper.

Gallina Alabaster

Land type: Mountainous forest.
GPS: N36° 14' 13" / W106° 51' 25".
Elevation: 7,340 feet.
Best time of year: April though October.
Land manager: New Mexico Department of Transportation.
Material: Alabaster, agate, and jasper.
Tools: Geological hammer, large shovel, sledgehammer, large pick, chisels, goggles, and gads.
Vehicle: Any vehicle is OK when it's dry, but four-wheel drive is recommended during wet periods.
Precautions and restrictions: Forest Road 76 can be very slippery when wet.
Special attractions: Abiquiu Reservoir boasts fine angling and scenery.
Finding the site: This alabaster area is located northeast of Cuba and southwest of the small town of Gallina. From the junction of U.S. Highway 550 and Highway 126 in Cuba, drive northwest on US 550 for 3.7 miles. Turn right (north) onto Highway 96 and continue for 12.9 miles to its junction with Highway 112, where Highway 96 makes a sharp turn to the right (east). Continue on Highway 96 for 4.1 miles, then turn right (south) onto FR 76 and drive up a steep hill.

Rockhounding

Though other guidebooks say that you have to drive a half mile to get to the alabaster, we found pieces up to 15 inches in diameter almost as soon as we drove up the hill, within 0.1 mile of Highway 96. The boulders appear to be eroding out of the top of the road cut. We also found some nice agates and jasper in the area.

Coyote

Land type: Mountainous forest.

GPS: N36° 10' 38" / W106° 41' 03" (junction of Highway 96 and Forest Road 172).

Elevation: 7,615 feet.

Best time of year: April through October.

Land manager: Santa Fe National Forest.

Material: Agate and petrified wood.

Tools: Geological hammer, small shovel, and spray bottle

Vehicle: Any vehicle is OK when it's dry; otherwise, four-wheel drive is needed.

Precautions and restrictions: These roads could be very muddy and slippery and may require four-wheel drive at times. Do not attempt to collect here if your vehicle can't handle wet conditions.

Special attractions: Abiquiu Reservoir boasts fine angling and scenery.

Finding the site: This area is west of the village of Coyote. From Coyote, drive west on Highway 96 for 4 miles and turn left (south) onto FR 172. This is the start of the collecting area. The road is paved for 0.2 mile, at which point it becomes gravel. Bear right here and continue south.

Rockhounding

We did not find a whole lot at this location, but we only drove about 3 miles, whereas the collecting area is reported to extend 10 miles. The GPS coordinates are for the place where we found the most material. It probably pays to drive farther into this collecting area, where the agate may be more abundant. Another road you may want to try is Forest Road 316, directly south out of Coyote. There have been reports of good agate-collecting along this road. Good luck—we hope you find more than we did.

Pedernal Peak

Land type: Mountainous forest.
GPS: N36° 10' 38" / W106° 32' 51".
Elevation: 7,115 feet.
Best time of year: April through October.
Land manager: Santa Fe National Forest.
Material: Agate.
Tools: Geological hammer, small shovel, spray bottle, sledgehammer, goggles, and chisels.
Vehicle: Any vehicle will do except in winter or wet weather, when four-wheel drive is required.
Precautions and restrictions: The forest road becomes very slippery when wet, so be sure your vehicle can handle it.
Special attractions: Abiquiu Reservoir boasts fine angling and scenery.
Finding the site: This area is located directly south of Youngsville. From Highway 96 on the eastern edge of Youngsville, proceed south on Forest Road 100,

The slopes around Pedernal Peak hold a lot of agate.

which takes you up the slopes of Pedernal Peak. Drive at least a mile before stopping to look for agate.

Rockhounding

The GPS coordinates were taken 1.6 miles after turning onto Forest Road 100, the first place we found abundant agate. You will see a lot of material here, most of it white with black inclusions and occasionally bright red swirls. Some of the agate is completely black. All this material is solid and takes a fine polish. You will find a variety of sizes, from tumblers to chunks large enough to make bookends. It appears that the average size of the agates increases as you drive farther up the road.

Abiquiu Dam

Land type: Mountainous desert.
GPS: N36° 14' 06" / W106° 25' 42".
Elevation: 6,370 feet.
Best time of year: March through November.
Land manager: New Mexico Department of Transportation.
Material: Agate and jasper.
Tools: Geological hammer, small shovel, goggles, and spray bottle.
Vehicle: Any.
Precautions and restrictions: Be careful walking along busy Highway 96, and park safely. Wear goggles when chipping.
Special attractions: Abiquiu Reservoir boasts fine angling and scenery.
Finding the site: This area is located northwest of Abiquiu. From the junction of U.S. Highway 84 and Highway 96, which is 6.5 miles northwest of the town of Abiquiu, drive west on Highway 96. It is 2.2 miles to the rest area on the

The agate area overlooking Abiquiu Reservoir.

north side of the road by the dam. The collecting area starts here and extends for quite a distance west on Highway 96.

Rockhounding

We found agate and jasper on the slope on the opposite (south) side of the road at the rest area, as well as walking along the right-of-way. You will find a rough path going up the mountain on the south side of the road. Follow this and keep an eye out for the agate. Much of this material is well worn and may be difficult to spot. Chip any suspect pieces.

We've heard reports of agates extending several miles west of the rest area. Much of this agate is similar to the variety found at Pedernal Peak; however, some may be considered moss. The rest area is a scenic place to have a picnic lunch or dinner.

Jemez Springs

Land type: Mountainous forest.
GPS: N35° 49' 36" / W106° 39' 14".
Elevation: 6,922 feet.
Best time of year: May through October.
Land manager: New Mexico Department of Transportation.
Material: Massive and crystal sulphur, obsidian in perlite, and marine fossils.
Vehicle: Any.
Tools: Geological hammer, sledgehammer, large pick, brush, goggles, respirator, and hand shovel.
Precautions and restrictions: The parking area here is very small, so you may want to find another spot and walk back to the site. Wear a mask and goggles when digging.
Special attractions: Observe 600-year-old pueblo ruins at Bandelier National Monument; camping is available. A number of private and public hot springs are located near Jemez Springs, in addition to the Soda Dam (see site 12).
Finding the site: This area is located directly north of Jemez Springs along Highway 4. From the Jemez Springs Post Office, drive 5.5 miles north on Highway 4 and park on the left (west) side next to a road cut.

Rockhounding

We found nice specimens of massive and crystal sulphur here. You will know you are at the right spot by the rotten egg smell that permeates the air—this is the sulphur aroma. The diggings are obvious. Pull out any chunks and brush them off to see if they contain crystals. We also found marine fossils and some obsidian nodules in the white perlite that is located right next to the sulphur diggings.

Soda Dam

Land type: Mountainous forest.
Best time of year: May through October.
Land manager: Santa Fe National Forest, Coyote Ranger District.
Material: Tufa.
Tools: None.
Vehicle: Any.
Precautions and restrictions: No collecting allowed. It might be difficult to park on busy days.
Special attractions: Observe 600-year-old pueblo ruins at Bandelier National Monument; camping is available. A number of private and public hot springs are located near Jemez Springs.
Finding the site: From Jemez Springs, drive 0.8 mile north on U.S. Highway 4.

Rockhounding

This is a natural dam formed by mineral deposits of calcium carbonate from the water of hot springs.

The Soda Dam is a very interesting geological feature.

Jemez Canyon

Land type: Mountainous forest.
GPS: N35° 49' 56" / W106° 38' 34".
Elevation: 6,919 feet.
Best time of year: March through October.
Land manager: New Mexico Department of Transportation.
Material: Marine fossils, including brachiopods, crinoid stems, and snails; calcite and quartz crystals.
Tools: Geological hammer and small shovel.
Vehicle: Any.
Precautions and restrictions: The parking area is small and narrow; be sure not to obstruct traffic. A larger pull-off can be found a little farther down the road on the left (east), where you can park and walk back. Be careful when proceeding up the slope in pursuit of fossils. It is composed of very loose shale and fossil remnants, and you may slide down, causing injury.
Special attractions: Observe 600-year-old pueblo ruins at Bandelier National Monument; camping is available. A number of private and public hot springs are located near Jemez Springs, in addition to the Soda Dam (see site 12).
Finding the site: This area is located directly north of Jemez Springs along Highway 4. From Jemez Springs, drive 6.3 miles north on Highway 4 and park on the left (west) side next to a large road cut.

Rockhounding

This is one of the best fossil locations we found in all of New Mexico. The collecting area continues north from the parking area for about another mile and south for at least 3 miles. The parking area road cut was the most prolific. We found all of the fossils listed above in both molds and casts, and some still had their original shells intact. If you are into fossil hunting, this is an easy must-go-to location. We also found chunks of calcite and quartz, which are quite common here.

Jemez Plateau Alabaster

Land type: Mountainous forest.

Best time of year: May through October.

Land manager: New Mexico Department of Transportation; Santa Fe National Forest.

Material: Alabaster-like material (might be tufa) and obsidian.

Tools: Geological hammer and small shovel.

Vehicle: Any.

Precautions and restrictions: Park well off the road and watch for traffic, as Highway 4 is a busy corridor.

Special attractions: Observe 600-year-old pueblo ruins at Bandelier National Monument; camping is available. A number of private and public hot springs are located near Jemez Springs, in addition to the Soda Dam (see site 12).

Finding the site: This area is located in the Santa Fe National Forest west of Los Alamos. From downtown Los Alamos at the junction of Diamond and Trinity, turn left (south) onto Diamond and continue 0.7 mile. Turn right (southwest) onto Highway 501 and drive 4.4 miles, then turn right (west) onto Highway 4 and continue another 14.8 miles to a pull-off on the left (south) side of the road.

Rockhounding

We found an easy cutting and carving material at this location. We think it's alabaster, but in any case, it carves well with a pocket knife. Look on the slope of the road cut on the right (north) side of the road. The pieces are not large, up to about 5 inches in diameter, which would be fine for small carvings.

Jemez Plateau Obsidian and Moonstone

Land type: Mountainous forest.
GPS: Site A: N35° 48' 55" / W106° 31' 59". Site B: N35° 49' 41" / W106° 35' 41".
Elevation: Site A: 8,419 feet. Site B: 8,160 feet.
Best time of year: May through October.
Land manager: Santa Fe National Forest.
Material: Obsidian, moonstone, and Apache tears.
Tools: Geological hammer, small shovel, and spray bottle.
Vehicle: Any.
Precautions and restrictions: Be very careful parking; stay well off the road. There are cougars and bears in the area, so take the proper precautions. Be aware of your surroundings before you hike too far off the road. Stay on the trails if you are not familiar with orienteering.
Special attractions: Observe 600-year-old pueblo ruins at Bandelier National Monument; camping is available. A number of private and public hot springs are located near Jemez Springs, in addition to the Soda Dam (see site 12).
Finding the site: This area is located in the Santa Fe National Forest southwest of Los Alamos. From downtown Los Alamos at the junction of Diamond and Trinity, turn left (south) onto Diamond and continue 0.7 mile. Turn right (southwest) onto Highway 501 and drive 4.4 miles, then turn right (west) onto Highway 4 and continue 13.5 miles to Las Conchas Trailhead. Park on the right (north) side to access site A. To get to site B, drive another 4.5 miles west and park at a large pull-off on the left (south) side. Site C is located another 3.2 miles west of site B.

Rockhounding

Much of this area was snow-covered when we were there in the middle of March. However, we were able to find some nice pieces of obsidian and Apache tears in the areas that were open.

A few Apache tears and a chunk of opaque but solid obsidian were picked up at site A. At site B giant boulders of snowflake obsidian were present in the road cut on the north side of the road, though much of this was too degraded to be useful for anything but display pieces. However, careful searching yielded a few nice pieces of beautiful snowflake and mahogany obsidian solid enough to cut. At site C look for a good pull-off on the left (south) side of the road—across from it is a large road cut, on the right (north) side. Snowflake obsidian and moonstone can be found here, and plenty more obsidian can be picked up in road cuts to the west of this area.

We also found one moonstone (⅛ inch) and a few other suspects. Moonstones up to ¼ inch have been reported in this area, but finding them might require more hiking and diligent searching. The best way to look for them is to get down close to the ground in any area of fine alluvial deposits or in the gravel of anthills. It's probably best to hunt for these gems on a sunny day, especially after a rain.

U.S. Highway 84 Road Cut (Mile 5.9)

Land type: High desert.
GPS: N36° 11' 30" / W106° 13' 46".
Elevation: 5,886 feet.
Best time of year: March through November.
Land manager: New Mexico Department of Transportation.
Material: Agate, petrified wood, and colorful quartzite.
Tools: Geological hammer, small shovel, and spray bottle.
Vehicle: Any.
Precautions and restrictions: Park well off the road, and be very careful of slides in the road cut.
Special attractions: Abiquiu Reservoir boasts fine angling and scenery. There are also trout streams in the area.
Finding the site: This area is just a short distance south of the village of Abiquiu. From Bodie's store in Abiquiu, follow U.S. Highway 84 south for 5.9 miles to a large road cut on the right (west).

Rockhounding

This road cut is a great source of small but colorful tumbling material. The agates and petrified wood we found were mostly white, clear, brown, or black. However, the quartzite was extremely colorful, with internal areas of yellow, red, and even blue and green.

We only give the location of one road cut, but similar material can probably be found in all such areas along US 84 and the surrounding the countryside. Some other places seem to have larger pieces.

La Madera Calcite

Land type: Mixed high desert and mountainous forest.
GPS: Site A: N36° 23' 41" / W106° 01' 26". Site B: N38° 23' 57" / W106° 01' 17".
Elevation: Site A: 7,358 feet. Site B: 7,512 feet.
Best time of year: May through October.
Land manager: New Mexico Department of Transportation.
Material: Calcite, garnet, agate, book mica, and pegmatite.
Tools: Geological hammer and small shovel.
Vehicle: Any.
Precautions and restrictions: Highway 519 is a dangerous road. Be sure to park safely.
Special attractions: The view of Tres Orejos and the Rio Grande Gorge from the rest area on Highway 68 about 8 miles south of Taos; the Rio Grande Gorge Visitor Center on Highway 68 in Pilar; and the hot springs at Ojo Caliente.

Nice books of mica can be picked up at La Madera mine.

Finding the site: This area is located north of the town of Ojo Caliente. From the Ojo Caliente Post Office, drive 2.2 miles northeast on U.S. Highway 285 to the junction of Highway 111. Turn left (north) onto Highway 111 and continue 3.3 miles to its junction with Highway 554. Continue straight on Highway 111 another 1.8 miles to the junction of Highway 519. Turn right (north) onto Highway 519 and drive another 1.4 miles to a pull-off on the right (east). Park here for site A. Site B is found at a hairpin curve on Highway 519 another 0.9 mile farther north.

Rockhounding

After parking at site A, climb down the bank and cross the wash to the mine area. The tailings from the mine are rather limited, but we picked up a few nice books of mica. Good specimens of mica in pegmatite will be evident. To get to the calcite, head up the path on the left. The calcite nodules and crystals are eroding out of the hillside. What's most interesting here is the calcite that has taken the form of book mica and has flat crystals. We also found a few garnets here.

Site B is a rock outcropping on the right (west) side of Highway 519, in the middle of the hairpin curve. Drive past it and turn right onto a dirt road, then park off this road and walk back to the outcropping. We found calcite as well as some really nice, though small, banded agate nodules. Some of these have crystal interiors.

La Madera Zeolites

Land type: Mountainous desert.

GPS: N36° 23' 56" / W106° 01' 10".

Elevation: 7,613 feet.

Best time of year: May through October.

Land manager: Carson National Forest.

Material: Heulandite and other zeolites, quartz crystals, calcite, and mordenite.

Tools: Geological hammer, small shovel, sledgehammer, chisels, gads, and goggles.

Vehicle: Any.

Precautions and restrictions: Stay off the road and beware of loose rocks above. Always wear goggles when hammering or chiseling.

Special attractions: The view of Tres Orejos and the Rio Grande Gorge from the rest area on Highway 68 about 8 miles south of Taos; the Rio Grand Gorge Visitor Center on Highway 68 in Pilar; and the hot springs at Ojo Caliente.

Finding the site: This area is located north of the town of Ojo Caliente. From the Ojo Caliente Post Office, drive 2.2 miles on U.S. Highway 285 to the junction of Highway 111. Turn left (north) onto Highway 111 and continue 3.3 miles to its junction with Highway 554. Continue straight on Highway 111 another 1.8 miles to the junction of Highway 519. Turn right (north) onto Highway 519 and drive for another 2.4 miles to a pull-off on the right (east). Park here.

Rockhounding

We found heulandite and other zeolites, quartz crystals, and calcite at this site. After parking, cross the road and walk 100 feet north. You will notice some loose basalt with white crystals. Sift through this stuff to get the specimens. You can also tackle the solid basalt with heavier equipment to expose the crystals. Although we didn't find it, mordenite has also been reported here.

La Madera Pegmatite

Land type: Mountainous desert.
GPS: N36° 24' 10" / W106° 01' 18".
Elevation: 7,357 feet.
Best time of year: May through October.
Land manager: New Mexico Department of Transportation.
Material: Mica, quartz, feldspar, and garnet.
Tools: Geological hammer, sledgehammer, chisels, gads, spray bottle, and goggles.
Vehicle: Any.
Precautions and restrictions: Highway 519 is very narrow and winding. Do not stop at the pegmatite and block the road. Keep an eye out for falling rocks.
Special attractions: The view of Tres Orejos and the Rio Grande Gorge from the rest area on Highway 68 about 8 miles south of Taos; the Rio Grand Gorge Visitor Center on Highway 68 in Pilar; and the hot springs at Ojo Caliente.
Finding the site: This area is located north of the town of Ojo Caliente. From the Ojo Caliente Post Office, drive 2.2 miles on U.S. Highway 285 to the junction of Highway 111. Turn left (north) onto Highway 111 and continue 3.3 miles to its junction with Highway 554. Continue straight on Highway 111 another 1.8 miles to the junction of Highway 519. Turn right (north) onto Highway 519 and drive another 2.6 miles to the pegmatite on the right (east) side of the road.

Rockhounding

The biggest problem with this site is that the parking is very limited. As you drive past the hairpin turn, look to the right—the pegmatite is quite obvious. It is bright white, while the surrounding rocks are gray/brown.

Pull in past the site, park, and then walk back. Nice books of mica can be chiseled out of the rocks. Colorful pink to salmon feldspar is also easy to get, and some of this polishes into nice moonstone-like gems. We also found some attractive red garnets in the quartz/feldspar matrix. This combination makes handsome display pieces.

Highway 519 Agate

Land type: Mixed forest and scrub desert.

GPS: N36° 24' 50" / W106° 00' 45".

Elevation: 7,036 feet.

Best time of year: May through October.

Land manager: Carson National Forest.

Material: Chalcedony roses, agate, rhyolite, and crystals.

Tools: Geological hammer, spray bottle, and small shovel.

Vehicle: Any.

Precautions and restrictions: You could be walking through brush here—think *snake* during warm weather.

Special attractions: The view of Tres Orejos and the Rio Grande Gorge from the rest area on Highway 68 about 8 miles south of Taos; the Rio Grand Gorge Visitor Center on Highway 68 in Pilar; and the hot springs at Ojo Caliente.

Finding the site: This area is located north of the town of Ojo Caliente. From the Ojo Caliente Post Office, drive 2.2 miles on U.S. Highway 285 to the junction of Highway 111. Turn left (north) onto Highway 111 and continue 3.3 miles to its junction with Highway 554. Continue straight on Highway 111 another 1.8 miles to the junction of Highway 519. Turn right (north) onto Highway 519 and drive for another 3.7 miles to the junction of Highway 341 on the right (east) side of the road. Turn right at this junction and immediately park at a large pull-off on the left (north).

Rockhounding

This location was a surprise, found when we stopped to eat lunch. We got out to look around, and to our delight, immediately spotted a beautiful translucent orange chalcedony rose. Banded agate was also picked up. We found some pieces of banded rhyolite with chalcedony roses still attached that make pretty display items. Some of the rhyolite also had eyes and would polish up into nice cabs.

A couple of the roses we found also display a bit of fire if you use your imagination, so keep an eye out for these precious gems. We only looked for about fifteen minutes and can only imagine what may be found here if one had some time.

Petaca Pegmatite Mines

Land type: Mountainous forest.

GPS: Site A: N36° 25' 46" / W106° 00' 40". Site B: N36° 30' 12" / W106° 01' 26".

Elevation: Site A: 7,033 feet. Site B: 7,034 feet.

Best time of year: June through September.

Land manager: Carson National Forest.

Material: Mica, quartz, beryl, garnet, feldspar, and tourmaline.

Tools: Geological hammer, sledgehammer, crowbar, chisels, gads, goggles, and spray bottle.

Vehicle: A heavy-duty two-wheel-drive vehicle will do most of the dry season, but four-wheel drive is preferred.

Precautions and restrictions: This is bear and cougar country, so take the appropriate precautions. Be sure your vehicle can make it up the road out of Petaca.

Special attractions: The view of Tres Orejos and the Rio Grande Gorge from the rest area on Highway 68 about 8 miles south of Taos; the Rio Grand Gorge Visitor Center on Highway 68 in Pilar; and the hot springs at Ojo Caliente.

Finding the site: This area is located north of the town of Ojo Caliente. From the Ojo Caliente Post Office, drive 2.2 miles on U.S. Highway 285 to the junction of Highway 111. Turn left (north) onto Highway 111 and continue 3.3 miles to its junction with Highways 554. Continue straight on Highway 111 another 1.8 miles to the junction of Highway 519. Turn right (north) onto Highway 519 and drive another 4.8 miles. You will see tracks heading off to the right (east) and the left (west)—this is site A. Pull off onto one of the sets of tracks and park.

To reach site B, continue on Highway 519 for 6 more miles to Petaca. Here your vehicle will probably be chased by a pack of territorial local dogs. They are harmless and appear to know what they're doing, so they won't get under your wheels. In Petaca, turn left (west) onto a gravel road, which is known as both County Road 0273 and Forest Road 45. Keep to the right at a fork while still in town, and follow this road 0.9 mile to where you will see a very rough road on the left coming in at a 45-degree angle. This road leads down to a mine and site B. Continue driving 0.1 mile and you will see the mine down the hill on the left (south). Do not park in the road; instead, drive another 0.2 mile to a good pull-off on the right (north).

Rockhounding

At site A old mines and tailings piles can be found on both sides of the road. Lots of mica and quartz, some of which would make nice display pieces, can be picked up. We also found just one small beryl crystal in the tailings on the left side after searching for about a half hour. Garnets and feldspar are also found in the area. To be more successful, you will have to do some heavy-duty hammering and chiseling. Tourmaline has been reported here, but we did not find any. Site B is about the same as site A.

In addition, about fifty other mines and prospects are located in the Petaca area, so if you have time, look around. Lots of big quartz boulders are spread around in the woods, and any of these may possess gems.

Tres Piedras

Land type: Very high and cold desert.
GPS: N36° 44' 43" / W105° 58' 55" (sign at beginning of road leading to mine).
Elevation: 8,178 feet.
Best time of year: May through October.
Land manager: New Mexico Department of Transportation; private.
Material: Apache tears and perlite.
Tools: Geological hammer and small shovel.
Vehicle: Any.
Precautions and restrictions: U.S. Highway 285 could be busy, so park appropriately.
Special attractions: The view of the Rio Grande Gorge from the US 64 bridge is incredible—it's like a little Grand Canyon.
Finding the site: This obsidian area is located north of Tres Piedras. From the junction of U.S. Highways 285 and 64, drive 6.9 miles north on US 285 to a

The Tres Piedras perlite mine is a good source of obsidian nodules.

pull-off on the right. This is just past the road to a large perlite mine, which will be visible on the right (east).

Rockhounding

The name of this mine is Dicapeal Corp. Perlite Mine, and it is located in No Agua, as indicated on the sign at the beginning of the road leading to the mine. Most of the property here is private, so your rockhounding either has to be confined to the right-of-way or you will need to get permission.

The Apache tears are the product of the erosion of perlite domes. They form the outer layers while the interior is pure perlite. We found some tears in a pile of dirt right on the shoulder of the road. While we only checked this one location, if you are in the area, definitely look at washes and other places where it is easy to pull off.

Crownpoint

Land type: Mountainous desert.
GPS: N35° 37' 21" / W108° 06' 40".
Elevation: 6,993 feet.
Best time of year: March though November.
Land manager: New Mexico Department of Transportation.
Material: Marine fossils, petrified wood, jasper, and selenite crystals.
Tools: Geological hammer, small shovel, and spray bottle.
Vehicle: Any.
Precautions and restrictions: Park well off the road, and watch the rocks above you when you are foraging around.
Special attractions: The Chaco Culture National Historical Park offers a look at the culture at the center of pueblo life between 850 and 1250 AD, in addition to camping, hiking, and a museum. Bisti Badlands (see site 1) and El Malpais National Monument (see site 26) are also nearby.
Finding the site: This area located south of Crownpoint and north of Thoreau on Highway 371. From Interstate 40 in Thoreau, take exit 53 north onto Highway 371. Continue on Highway 371 to a large pull-off on the right (east) side of the road.

Rockhounding

This was one of those serendipitous finds. We parked in the pull-off late one evening while doing research for this book. In the morning, while walking the dogs, we noticed some fossil molds lying around in the rocks in the parking area.

The road cut is on the west side across from the pull-off. Examining the area, we found some more molds, fine casts, a few pieces of petrified wood, jasper, chert, and some beautiful selenite desert roses. If you want to get the roses home intact, be sure to bring plenty of soft packaging—they are very fragile.

Thoreau

Land type: Flat high desert.
GPS: N35° 23' 23" / W108° 11' 07".
Elevation: 7,047 feet.
Best time of year: March through November.
Land manager: New Mexico Department of Transportation.
Material: Petrified wood, agate, and jasper.
Tools: Geological hammer and small shovel.
Vehicle: Any.
Precautions and restrictions: Highway 122 could be busy, so park well off the pavement.
Special attractions: The Chaco Culture National Historical Park offers a look at the culture at the center of pueblo life between 850 and 1250 AD, in addition to camping, hiking, and a museum. Bisti Badlands (see site 1) and El Malpais National Monument (see site 26) are also nearby.
Finding the site: This area is located directly east of the town of Thoreau. From Interstate 40, take exit 53 to Thoreau, which will put you on Highway 371 north. Immediately, take the first right (east) onto Highway 122, which parallels I-40. The collecting area begins after 1 mile and extends for approximately 5 miles.

Rockhounding

Nothing is very abundant here. We found a few nice pieces of petrified wood (including a limb cast), an agate, and three pieces of jasper. These were all small but good for tumbling. In this area you are limited to the right-of-way due to private land on the north and the highway on the south. If you put in enough time, however, a nice bag full of pretty pieces can be collected. The GPS coordinates are for the best place we stopped, which was at mile 1.7 of the collecting area. We did not have time to go farther, so perhaps a more abundant site can be located.

Grants Ridge

Land type: Mountainous desert.
GPS: N35° 11' 59" / W107° 45' 26".
Elevation: 7,092 feet.
Best time of year: March through October.
Land manager: Bureau of Land Management, Albuquerque District; Cibola National Forest.
Material: Apache tears, rhyolite, topaz, and garnet.
Tools: Geological hammer, sledgehammer, chisel, gads, crowbar, and goggles.
Vehicle: Any.
Precautions and restrictions: Always wear goggles and protective clothing when chiseling—you want to be able to appreciate what you find.
Special attractions: El Malpais National Monument (see site 26).
Finding the site: This area is located northeast of Grants. From Grants, take exit 81 north off Interstate 40. Drive 0.1 mile to U.S. Highway 66 and turn right (east). Follow US 66 for 1.5 miles to First Street, turn left (north), and travel 0.8 mile. Make a right (east) and travel another 0.4 mile, at which point the road becomes Highway 547. Turn left (north), continuing on Highway 547, and you will see Lobo Canyon Shopping Center on the right (east). Drive another 5.3 miles to a pull-off on the left (west) and park here. At this point you will see Grants Ridge on the left (west). Hike down the path toward the ridge.

Rockhounding

This is hard work—rocks have to be split and the crystals gently chiseled out. Plus, you have to think small. While others have reported garnets and topaz crystals up to an inch, the largest we found were more like ½ inch. The GPS coordinates are for the first place we found garnet.

Simply pick up rocks that look vuggy, then split them and examine what is inside. Most have both garnets and topaz and a few other minerals that we have not yet identified, such as the long black crystals with some chatoyance and another that looks like labradorite to us. Finding Apache tears is a little easier— just walk around and pick them up. The rhyolite we found is banded and quite pretty. It takes a good polish and makes fine jewelry and decorative pieces such as bookends.

El Malpais National Monument

Land type: High desert.
Best time of year: All year.
Land manager: El Malpais National Monument.
Material: Basalt.
Tools: None.
Vehicle: Two-wheel drive.
Precautions and restrictions: No collecting allowed.
Finding the site: El Malpais is located south of Grants and can be reached via Interstate 40. Take exit 89, east of Grants, onto Highway 117. This forms the eastern boundary. The El Malpais National Monument ranger station is located 9 miles south of this exit, just off Highway 117, and is open daily.

Rockhounding

This is a giant area of lava flows and a must-see for anyone interested in geological processes. A number of hiking trails make it easy to get up close to the rocks.

Lava flows at El Malpais National Monument.

Rio Puerco Zeolites and Calcite Crystals

Land type: High desert.
GPS: N35° 02' 10" / W106° 56' 21".
Elevation: 5,268 feet.
Best time of year: February through May, October, and November.
Land manager: New Mexico Department of Transportation.
Material: Zeolites, calcite, agate, jasper, and petrified wood.
Tools: Geological hammer, sledgehammer, chisel, gads, goggles, and crowbar.
Vehicle: Any.
Precautions and restrictions: Always wear goggles when chiseling. In fact, it is also a good idea to wear protective gloves and clothing.
Special attractions: The New Mexico Museum of Natural History and Science is a wonderful natural history museum with an emphasis on New Mexico. The Maxwell Museum of Anthropology has exhibits reflecting the entire history of humankind, with an emphasis on the Southwest. There are many other very good museums in and around Albuquerque.
Finding the site: Take Interstate 40 west from Albuquerque to exit 140 at Rio Puerco, which will put you on the frontage road heading west. Drive 0.1 mile to a service station and turn right immediately before it. Continue past the convenience store, then drive across a cattle guard and park.

Rockhounding

After you park, you will see a large mesa with big boulders scattered at the bottom. Walk to the mesa while keeping an eye out for pieces of agate, jasper, and petrified wood. The mesa is old basalt with many pockets filled with zeolites and calcite crystals, and it takes a lot of chipping, prying, and hammering to remove the specimens intact. It is, however, well worth the effort. You can also just pick up some smaller rocks with calcite and zeolites. During the short time we were there, we found a small piece that contained garnets.

There may be private property issues in the area. Be sure you don't enter private land without permission. If you are worried about trespassing, notice where the lava flow comes close to the frontage road. You can collect there in the right-of-way.

Rio Puerco Agate and Jasper

Land type: High desert.

GPS: Site A: N35° 02' 10" / W106° 56' 21". Site B: N35° 02' 15" / W106° 55' 31".

Elevation: Site A: 5,268 feet. Site B: 5,327 feet.

Best time of year: February through May, October, and November.

Land manager: New Mexico Department of Transportation.

Material: Agate, jasper, quartzite, and petrified wood.

Tools: Geological hammer, small shovel, and spray bottle.

Vehicle: Any.

Precautions and restrictions: Be sure to park well off the road at site B, as it is quite busy. Watch for private property.

Special attractions: The New Mexico Museum of Natural History and Science is a wonderful natural history museum with an emphasis on New Mexico. The Maxwell Museum of Anthropology has exhibits reflecting the entire history of humankind, with an emphasis on the Southwest. There are many other very good museums in and around Albuquerque.

Finding the site: Take Interstate 40 west from Albuquerque to exit 140 at Rio Puerco, which will put you on the frontage road heading west. Drive 0.1 mile to a service station and turn right immediately before it. Continue past the convenience store, then go across a cattle guard and park. This is the beginning of site A. To get to site B, exit the interstate, then turn around and drive east along the frontage road, which parallels the interstate. Drive past the exit and stop anywhere for the next couple miles.

Rockhounding

The GPS coordinates for site A were taken at the first parking area. After parking your vehicle at site A, walk north on the gravel road, which leads to a flying field for ultralight aircraft a few miles ahead. Walk through the gate and past the second cattle guard. You are now on Abrams Road, and agate, petrified wood, and jasper of many varieties can be found all along it. Some of the pieces found are substantial in size and quite solid, and are therefore good for cutting. Besides the chalcedony, we found some very colorful quartzite pieces, which cut and polish well. Plenty of tumbling-size pieces can also be picked up.

You might be surrounded by private land, so be sure not to trespass. However, plenty of material can be found right along the corridor, so it is not necessary to enter private land. Each time the road is graded, a wealth of new material is brought to the surface. Some of these stones are very weathered and require chipping to be sure of what you have.

At site B more of the same stones can be found, but they are smaller and less numerous. These are more appropriate for tumbling as opposed to cutting. The GPS coordinates are for a point a mile east of the gas station, but keep in mind that plenty can be picked up anywhere you stop within the given parameters. When we were there, the land on the north side of the road was fenced in and the gate was locked, which probably indicates that it is private. However, the right-of-way is quite large on both sides, and plenty of material can be found without trespassing.

Albuquerque, 98th Street

Land type: High desert.

GPS: N35° 05' 47" / W106° 45' 12".

Elevation: 5,269 feet.

Best time of year: February through May, October, and November.

Land manager: New Mexico Department of Transportation.

Material: Agate and jasper.

Tools: Geological hammer, small shovel, and spray bottle.

Vehicle: Any.

Precautions and restrictions: Be aware of private property, and park so as not to block traffic.

Special attractions: The New Mexico Museum of Natural History and Science is a wonderful natural history museum with an emphasis on New Mexico. The Maxwell Museum of Anthropology has exhibits reflecting the entire history of humankind, with an emphasis on the Southwest. There are many other very good museums in and around Albuquerque.

Finding the site: Some nice agates can be found on the western edge of the Albuquerque city limits. From downtown Albuquerque, drive west on Interstate 40 to exit 153 (98th Street exit). Follow 98th Street north to the end of the pavement, which is 0.6 mile from where you exited I-40. The street continues as a gravel road. Park anywhere on the side.

Rockhounding

When you park and get out of your vehicle, the agates will be apparent almost immediately. Most of them are clear and white, with all kinds of interesting inclusions. We also found some that are banded.

The land on the west side of the road appears to be open, but when we were there, development was taking place on the east side. This is prime real estate in the Albuquerque suburbs, and the collecting status will probably change rapidly. Before getting to the end of the pavement, you will notice large power lines and a power line road to the left (west). This area will probably remain open for a while.

Los Lunas

Land type: High desert.

GPS: N34° 43' 56" / W106° 52' 55".

Elevation: 5,223 feet.

Best time of year: February through May, October, and November.

Land manager: Bureau of Land Management, Albuquerque District.

Material: Agate, jasper, petrified wood, quartzite, carnelian, and obsidian.

Tools: Geological hammer, small shovel, and spray bottle.

Vehicle: Four-wheel drive.

Precautions and restrictions: This is a very remote area. Make sure your vehicle is in good shape and that you carry enough water and fuel to get out of trouble.

Special attractions: The New Mexico Museum of Natural History and Science is a wonderful natural history museum with an emphasis on New Mexico. The Maxwell Museum of Anthropology has exhibits reflecting the entire history of humankind, with an emphasis on the Southwest. There are many other very good museums in and around Albuquerque.

Finding the site: This prolific area is located 25 miles south of Albuquerque. From Albuquerque, drive south on Interstate 25 to exit 203 (Los Lunas exit). Head west on Highway 6 for 4.7 miles and turn left (south) onto a road right after the Sheldon Horse Adoption Center, which is on the left (south). Continue on this well-graded road, which parallels railroad tracks for 3.3 miles, and cross a different set of railroad tracks. At this point you will see a tall radio tower on the right (west) and a road going off to the left (east). Bear right (west), following the set of railroad tracks you just crossed. Go another 0.5 mile to another radio tower on the left (south). At this point the road turns gradually toward the west, still paralleling the railroad tracks. After another 0.4 mile, the road forks. Take the left fork and drive south. After 1.1 miles on this new road, you will pass between two buildings with no trespassing signs. Continue on this road, which twists and turns but generally heads in a southerly direction, for 0.9 mile. At this point you will come to a T. Turn right (west) and drive another 0.4 mile. Here another road comes in on the right (north). Continue past this road in a southwesterly direction for 0.7 mile to another T. Park anywhere around here.

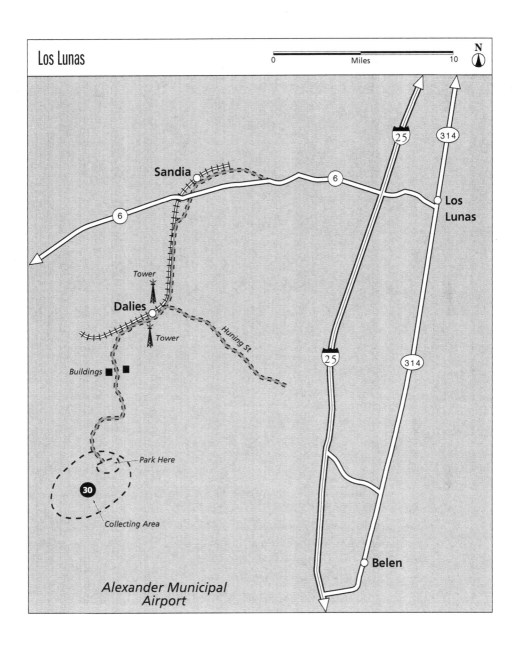

Los Lunas

0 — Miles — 10

N

Sandia

6

6

25

314

Los
Lunas

Tower

Dalies

Huning St

Tower

25

314

Buildings ■ ■

Park Here

30

Collecting Area

Belen

*Alexander Municipal
Airport*

Most of the stones found at Los Lunas are either agates, petrified wood, or nice quartzite.

Rockhounding

This is a very prolific area, but difficult to get to. It took us the better part of a half day to find the site; however, it was a worthwhile endeavor. Follow our directions precisely, and constantly refer to the accompanying map.

After parking at the given location, agate, petrified wood, and jasper will be evident all around you. Walk in any direction and start collecting. So much is here that it becomes difficult to decide what to keep. The agates range in color from clear and white to black, yellow, gold, and red. Some have plume patterns, while others are filled with moss, and a few of the pieces will be nicely banded.

The wood is also rather diverse. Some chunks are colorful, but most are gray, clear, brown, and white. Many are nicely patterned, and most are quite solid. In addition, we found some colorful, nicely patterned quartzite. Don't neglect this material—it makes fine cut pieces. We also found a few small fragments of obsidian and carnelian.

Please do not collect more than you can use. Leave some specimens for future rockhounds.

Northeastern New Mexico

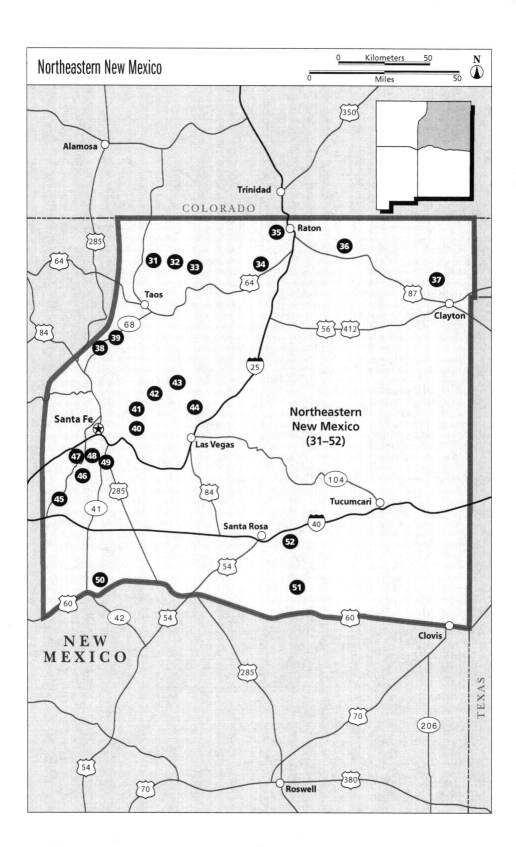

Northeastern New Mexico

Alamosa

Trinidad

COLORADO

285

64

Raton **35**

36

31 **32** **33**   **34**

Taos   64   87 **37**

68   Clayton

84   56   412

39

38   25

43

42

41   **44**   Northeastern
New Mexico
(31–52)

Santa Fe   **40**

Las Vegas

47 **48**   104

46   **49**

285   84   Tucumcari

45

41   Santa Rosa   40

52

50   54

60   **51**

42   54   60   Clovis

NEW
MEXICO

285   TEXAS

70

206

54

70   380   Roswell

Questa

Land type: Mountainous forest.

GPS: Site A: N36° 41' 08" / W105° 32' 11". Site B: N36° 40' 56" / W105° 30' 38".

Elevation: Site A: 8,180 feet. Site B: 7,872 feet.

Best time of year: April through October.

Land manager: New Mexico Department of Transportation.

Material: Molybdite, molybdenite, chalcopyrite, feldspar, serpentine, calcite, rhodochrosite, pyrite, sphalerite, and fluorite.

Tools: Geological hammer.

Vehicle: Any.

Precautions and restrictions: Park well off the road, and use caution while collecting next to it. The mine itself is off-limits without permission.

Special attractions: Coyote Creek State Park and Cimarron Canyon State Park have fishing, hiking, camping, and wildlife viewing. The E. I. Couse Historic Home and Studio and the Millicent Rogers Museum are both nearby in Taos.

Finding the site: This giant mine is east of the town of Questa. From the junction of Highways 522 and 38 in Questa, go east on Highway 38 for 3.9 miles. Pull off the road and park for site A. Drive another 1.6 miles east on Highway 38 to site B.

Rockhounding

The mining area between Questa and Red River is extensive. The dumps go on and on for many miles—almost the entire distance between the two towns. We give two sites, but please do not confine your search to just them.

There appear to be two types of dumps: the yellow ones and the gray ones. We only found molybdite in the yellow dumps, but that does not mean that other minerals are not present. Molybdenite, chalcopyrite, feldspar, serpentine, and calcite were found in the gray areas. Site A is yellow, and site B is gray.

Pyrite, sphalerite, and fluorite have also been reported from this area in addition to rhodochrosite, which we really wanted to find but it was not in the cards. Perhaps if you spend enough time or get lucky, a chunk of this beautiful material will be gracing your collection. Please leave some for our next trip!

Red River

Land type: Mountainous forest.
GPS: Site A: N36° 41' 18" / W105° 23' 02". Site B: N36° 41' 55" / W105° 22' 59".
Elevation: Site A: 8,855 feet. Site B: 9,195 feet.
Best time of year: June through September.
Land manager: Carson National Forest.
Material: Feldspar and marine fossils.
Tools: Geological hammer, small shovel, sifter, sledgehammer, chisel, and goggles.
Vehicle: Any vehicle is usually OK, but if the roads are wet or icy, even a four-wheel drive could be dangerous.
Precautions and restrictions: The road at site A could be very slippery, and the mountain drops off right at its edge. Be sure you know your vehicle's limits. Site B is a very busy road, so park well off the pavement. Also, the road cut is very steep and rocky. Watch for loose rocks from above.
Special attractions: Coyote Creek State Park and Cimarron Canyon State Park have fishing, hiking, camping, and wildlife viewing. The E. I. Couse Historic Home and Studio and the Millicent Rogers Museum are both nearby in Taos.
Finding the site: This area is located east of the town of Red River. From the junction of Highways 38 and 578 in Red River, turn south on Highway 578 and go 1.1 miles, then make a left (southeast) onto Red River Pass Road. Drive 0.3 mile to a pull-off on your left (east), which is site A. To get to site B, again starting at the junction of Highways 38 and 578 in Red River, drive east on Highway 38 for 1.3 miles to a large road cut on the left (north). Park on the left side of the road.

Rockhounding

Feldspar crystals can be found at both sites. You can drive partway up the dirt road at site A, even with two-wheel drive, but if it is wet or icy, even a four-wheel-drive vehicle could be dangerous.

We found a few very good-looking feldspar crystals in a monzonite matrix at site A. They are very difficult to extract but would make nice display pieces if left in the country rock. Though not lucky enough to find any ourselves, we have heard that at times these crystals can be found loose in the rubble at the base of the slides along Red River Pass Road. We were there in mid-March, and the road was snow-covered above the point we drove to. The rockhounding is supposed to get better the farther you go up the hill.

We found some more monzonite with internal crystals at site B. Also look in the small rubble piles at the base of the cliffs to see if any loose crystals are present. While we did not find any in the five minutes spent looking, you might be luckier than we were. We did find marine fossils at both sites.

Highway 38 Lepidolite

Land type: Mountainous forest.
GPS: N36° 40' 47" / W105° 20' 05".
Elevation: 9,163 feet.
Best time of year: June through September.
Land manager: New Mexico Department of Transportation.
Material: Lepidolite and other micas, granite, and serpentine.
Tools: Geological hammer and small shovel.
Vehicle: Any.
Precautions and restrictions: Stopping directly in front of the road cut could be dangerous, so be sure to park where we describe. Beware of loose rocks above you.
Special attractions: Coyote Creek State Park and Cimarron Canyon State Park have fishing, hiking, camping, and wildlife viewing. The E. I. Couse Historic Home and Studio and the Millicent Rogers Museum are both nearby in Taos.
Finding the site: This area is located east of Red River. From the junction of Highways 38 and 578 in the town of Red River, follow Highway 38 east for 5.7 miles. You will see a large road cut on the left (north). A pull-off is found on the right (south) after passing the road cut.

Rockhounding

We found lepidolite and other micas, granite, and serpentine at this site. If it is sunny, the bright red/pink/purple color of this road cut will jump into your eyes as you drive past. The granite is extremely pretty because much of the mica in it is lepidolite. It polishes very well and makes beautiful jewelry and other decorative pieces. Some of the fragments also make very handsome display items, especially if your cabinet is lighted.

U.S. Highway 64 Rhyolite

Land type: High desert.
GPS: N36° 44' 27" / W104° 30' 57".
Elevation: 6,347 feet.
Best time of year: March through October.
Land manager: New Mexico Department of Transportation.
Material: Banded rhyolite.
Tools: Geological hammer and small shovel.
Vehicle: Any.
Precautions and restrictions: Though the highway is wide, it could be busy. Park well off the pavement.
Special attractions: There are two interesting museums across the border in Trinidad, Colorado: the A. R. Mitchell Memorial Museum and Gallery, which features Western art, and the Trinidad History Museum. Also in the vicinity are Capulin Volcano National Monument (see site 36) and Clayton Lake State Park (see site 37).
Finding the site: This area is located southwest of Raton. From Raton, take Interstate 25 south to exit 446 and U.S. Highway 64. Follow US 64 west 6.7 miles to a road cut and park on the shoulder.

Rockhounding

This was another of those serendipitous finds. We were driving along on a beautiful sunny day in March, and it was time to walk the dogs. When we got out of the camper, a beautiful banded piece of a nodule was sitting right next to the door. The bands ranged from yellow to red to brown to cream to white to rust. At first we thought the piece was agate/jasper, but upon closer inspection, its rhyolite nature became apparent. What was most unusual was that the piece was obviously from a nodule that had a hollow center—a smooth interior, no crystals.

You will find plenty of small pieces at this site. Some are solid red, while others are completely yellow. A few will exhibit banding. But don't confine your search to the particular road cut we describe. This material can be found in most of the right-of-way for a number of miles. In fact, some of this stuff appears to be eroding out of a layer of rock just as you go under the railroad tracks as you drive east. We never found a complete nodule, but perhaps you will.

Raton

Land type: Hilly city.
GPS: N36° 54' 18" / W104° 26' 36".
Elevation: 6,765 feet.
Best time of year: March through October.
Land manager: New Mexico Department of Transportation.
Material: Marine fossils, plant fossils, and leaf imprints.
Tools: Geological hammer, small shovel, and screwdriver or small chisel.
Vehicle: Any.
Precautions and restrictions: This site is within the city limits, so be careful where you park.
Special attractions: There are two interesting museums across the border in Trinidad, Colorado: the A. R. Mitchell Memorial Museum and Gallery, which features Western art, and the Trinidad History Museum. Also in the vicinity are Capulin Volcano National Monument (see site 36) and Clayton Lake State Park (see site 37).
Finding the site: This fossil area is located on the west side of the city of Raton. From Interstate 25, take exit 451 west onto U.S. Highway 64/87 (Clayton Road). Drive 1.8 miles and turn right (north) onto Business I-25, which eventually becomes Second Street. Continue into the downtown area on this road for 1.3 miles and turn left (west) on Savage Street. Follow this street 0.2 mile to a T. This is North Fifth Avenue. Make a left (south) and park.

Rockhounding

The described location is only one of many around Raton. Any place you can get close to the mesas within view of the city, fossils will probably be found.

At this site you will see a flag on top of a steep hill. Any piece of rubble on the slope holds the potential for fossils; however, it appears that the best rocks to look in are the cherty ones. We found nice marine fossils as well as what appear to be casts of tree stems. Leaf imprints are reported to be in this area, but we did not find any. We only spent about a half hour looking, so perhaps with more time and luck, they can be found.

Capulin Volcano National Monument

Land type: Desert and forest.
Elevation: 8,182 feet.
Best time of year: April through October.
Land manager: Capulin Volcano National Monument.
Material: Volcanic.
Tools: None.
Vehicle: Any.
Precautions and restrictions: No collecting allowed.
Finding the site: The park is located 33 miles east of Raton. From Raton, take U.S. Highway 64/87 about 30 miles to Capulin. Turn left (north) onto Highway 325 and drive 3 miles to the park entrance.

Rockhounding

This national monument is of significant geological interest. About 60,000 years ago an eruption created Capulin Volcano, which rises more than 1,000 feet above the surrounding desert and is a nearly perfectly shaped cinder cone. Stretching about a mile in circumference, the crater is around 400 feet deep. This is one of the best places to observe and understand volcanic processes.

Capulin Volcano National Monument is a great place for rockhounding.

Clayton Lake State Park

Land type: Rolling grassland.

Elevation: 5,040 feet.

Best time of year: April through October.

Material: Fossils.

Land manager: Clayton Lake State Park.

Tools: None.

Vehicle: Any.

Special attractions: The park offers hiking, excellent fishing, camping, wildlife viewing, and boating.

Precautions and restrictions: No collecting allowed.

Finding the site: From Clayton, take Highway 370 (Lake Road) north for about 10 miles to Highway 455 west and follow it to the park.

Rockhounding

This park sports more than 500 dinosaur footprints from various carnivores and plant-eaters. In addition, some prints of ancient crocodiles have been preserved and identified. Don't miss the interpretive trail with markers that identify significant tracks and paleontological features, but try to take the walk in the cool of the morning or late afternoon.

Harding Pegmatite Mine

Land type: Mountainous forest.

GPS: N36° 11' 38" / W105° 47' 28".

Elevation: 7,359 feet.

Best time of year: May through October.

Land manager: University of New Mexico.

Material: Lepidolite, feldspar, quartz, cleavelandite, tantalite, garnet, beryl, muscovite, albite, amazonite, spodumene, apatite, calcite, and microlite.

Tools: Geological hammer, chisels, gads, goggles, spray bottle, and large and small shovels.

Vehicle: Any.

Precautions and restrictions: Do not enter the area without a permit. The final road can get muddy during wet periods.

Special attractions: The view of Tres Orejos and the Rio Grande Gorge from the rest area on Highway 68 about 8 miles south of Taos should not be missed. Learn about the geologic and natural history of the area at the Rio Grande Gorge Visitor Center, located on Highway 68 in Pilar. The Upper Rio Grande has good fishing and rafting.

Finding the site: This prolific mine is located southwest of Taos. From the junction of Highways 518 and 68 at Ranchos de Taos, travel southwest on Highway 68 for 13.4 miles to the Rio Grande Gorge Visitor Center in Pilar. From there, continue 8.1 miles and turn left (east) on Highway 75. Drive 1.9 miles to the Dixon Community Store on the right, then continue another 2.9 miles to the Rio Arriba–Taos county line. In another 3.5 miles you will see two roads leading off to the south on the right. Take the second sandy road, drive 0.4 mile to the mine entrance, and park.

Rockhounding

This is must-go-to for any serious mineral collector. Those who like to cut and polish will appreciate the lepidolite and solid pink feldspar. For mineral collectors, the variety and quantity of material is perhaps greater here than at any other location in New Mexico. We found lepidolite, feldspar, quartz, cleavelandite, tantalite, garnet, beryl, and muscovite, while others have reported albite, amazonite, spodumene, apatite, calcite, and microlite.

The Harding Pegmatite Mine is the source of many different minerals.

You must get a permit before entering the pegmatite area. At the time of this writing, permits were obtainable from Gilbert Griego, Harding Mine, P.O. Box 271, Dixon, NM 87527, gilgriego@windstream.net, or from the Department of Geology at the University of New Mexico in Albuquerque. The forms can also be downloaded at http://epswww.unm.edu/harding/release/relform.htm and mailed in. At present a $50 fee applies for groups of ten or more and a donation is requested from individuals. If the gate is locked, you will have to go hunt down Mr. Griego.

Picuris Mountains

Land type: Mountainous forest.
GPS: N36° 17' 51" / W105° 43' 19".
Elevation: 7,181 feet.
Best time of year: May through October.
Land manager: Carson National Forest.
Material: Staurolite crystals and garnet.
Tools: Geological hammer and screwdriver.
Vehicle: Any vehicle will do if you park at the beginning of the gravel road; otherwise, a rugged high-clearance four-wheel drive is necessary.
Precautions and restrictions: The gravel road is extremely rough. Don't attempt driving it if your vehicle is not in top-notch condition. Also know your limits if you are hiking.
Special attractions: The view of Tres Orejos and the Rio Grande Gorge from the rest area on Highway 68 about 8 miles south of Taos should not be missed. Learn about the geologic and natural history of the area at the Rio Grande Gorge Visitor Center, located on Highway 68 in Pilar. The Upper Rio Grande has good fishing and rafting.
Finding the site: This location is southwest of Taos. From the junction of Highways 518 and 68 at Ranchos de Taos, travel southwest on Highway 68 for 9 miles. You will see a gravel road off to the left (east) with a small pull-off. Park here.

Rockhounding

We hiked in about 0.7 mile along this rough road. In an hour of searching, we found only one staurolite crystal: a 1-inch, 60/120-degree fairy cross in a schist matrix. They may not be easy to come by, but if you spend enough time, a few can be located.

We heard reports that the area becomes more prolific the farther you hike in. You may want to take off from the road and keep your eyes open for micaceous soil and schist containing garnets. This is prime staurolite territory. If you do this, you should have a good compass, or better yet, a GPS device. Getting lost in the thick forest is easy to do. You also have to be in good physical condition because the area is quite steep.

This entire mountain range is known for staurolite, so there's no telling where you might find some. Any exposure of schist from the Rio Arriba–Taos county line as far as Rancho de Taos could be a source of fairy crosses. So if you have some time, do a bit of exploring. We're sure you'll find that perfect fairy cross if you put in enough time.

Pecos

Land type: Mountainous forest.
GPS: Site A: N35° 35' 37" / W105° 40' 48". Site B: N35° 35' 57" / W105° 40' 47".
Elevation: Site A: 7,004 feet. Site B: 7,005 feet.
Best time of year: May through October.
Land manager: New Mexico Department of Transportation.
Material: Marine fossils.
Tools: Geological hammer, small shovel, and heavy-duty screwdriver or small chisel.
Vehicle: Any.
Precautions and restrictions: Park well off the road, as it can be busy. Beware of rocks that might fall from above, and if you walk up the banks, watch for slippery areas.

A fossil clam eroding out of the road at the Pecos fossil site.

Special attractions: The state fish hatchery welcomes visitors to its facility on the left (west) side of Highway 63, just past the monastery on the left and the fossil-collecting road cuts on the right.

There is good trout fishing in the Pecos River, which more or less parallels this road. Many anglers also try their luck in Monastery Lake.

Finding the site: This area is northeast of Santa Fe. From Santa Fe, take Interstate 25 north to exit 299. After exiting, turn right (east) onto Highway 50 and drive 5.9 miles to Highway 63. Go north on Highway 63 through the village of Pecos. Site A is at a road cut on the right (east) side of the road in 1.5 miles. Site B is 0.3 mile farther on the same side.

Rockhounding

We found a wide variety of marine fossil impressions in the rocks at site A, and more of the same at site B. In addition, some very large clams can be seen eroding out of the bank. These can be easily removed using a screwdriver.

Terrero (Pecos) Mine

Land type: Mountainous forest.
GPS: N35° 45' 29" / W105° 40' 16".
Elevation: 7,846 feet.
Best time of year: May through October.
Land manager: New Mexico Department of Transportation.
Material: Chalcopyrite, argentiferous galena, bornite, hematite, garnet, pyrite, mica, actinolite, tourmaline, and lepidolite.
Tools: Small shovel, geological hammer, and spray bottle.
Vehicle: Any.
Precautions and restrictions: Parking is a problem here because the road is narrow and winding. You are better off walking a bit than parking and obstructing traffic.
Special attractions: The state fish hatchery welcomes visitors to its facility on the left (west) side of Highway 63, just past the monastery on the left and the fossil-collecting road cuts on the right.

There is good trout fishing in the Pecos River, which more or less parallels this road. Many anglers also try their luck in Monastery Lake.

Finding the site: This mine is located about 14 miles north of the village of Pecos. From Santa Fe, take Interstate 25 north to exit 299. After exiting, turn right (east) onto Highway 50 and drive 5.9 miles to Highway 63. Go north on Highway 63 through the village of Pecos and continue another 13.5 miles to the Terrero Store. Continue 1.6 miles past the store to a pull-off on the right (east).

Rockhounding

This mine is being reclaimed by the state and is posted. However, rockhounds can still find some nice specimens by looking through the portion of the dumps that come down to the road. The GPS coordinates are for the farthest extent of the tailings where there is a good pull-off. We also stopped at a small pull-off on the right (west) a few tenths of a mile as you head back south. Nice specimens were found across the road on the west side. We found chalcopyrite, argentiferous galena, bornite, hematite, and garnets in the area, while others have reported pyrite, mica, actinolite, tourmaline, and lepidolite.

You'd better get here soon if you intend to collect at this mine. It will probably become more and more difficult in the future, but that shouldn't stop you from trying.

Rociada

Land type: Mountainous forest.
GPS: Site A: N35° 51' 56" / W105° 29' 28". Site B: N35° 51' 55" / W105° 29' 28".
Elevation: Site A: 8,995 feet. Site B: 9,030 feet.
Best time of year: May through September.
Land manager: Bureau of Land Management, Farmington District.
Material: Lepidolite, garnet, apricot quartz, and green mica.
Tools: Geological hammer, small shovel, spray bottle, goggles, sledgehammer, chisels, gads, and crowbar.
Vehicle: Any vehicle will do if you hike the last 1.1 miles; otherwise, a high-clearance four-wheel drive is necessary.
Precautions and restrictions: A big mine shaft is located at site B. Be very careful around the structures, as lots of rusty nails are sticking out of the boards. Always wear goggles when chiseling; protective gloves and clothing are also a good idea. If you hike, know your limits. Bears and cougars in the area, so take the proper precautions.
Special attractions: Storrie Lake State Park has fishing, hiking, wildlife viewing, and camping. The Rough Rider Memorial collection at the City of Las Vegas Museum is great. The pools at Montezuma Hot Springs, located 6 miles northwest of Las Vegas on Highway 65, are free and the setting is beautiful.
Finding the site: This mine is located northwest of Las Vegas. From Interstate 25, take Las Vegas exit 345 west. Turn right onto Business I-25 and drive a few hundred yards to Mills Road, then turn left (west) and drive another mile to Highway 518. Continue north to Sapello on Highway 518 past Storrie Lake and the dam, which is on the left (west), for a total of 11.6 miles. In Sapello, turn left (northwest) onto Highway 94 and drive another 8.7 miles to Tierra Monte and Highway 105. Turn west (left) and drive 3.5 miles to a fork. A trash bin is on the right. Take the left fork (Highway 276) toward Lower Rociada and drive through the town, past the end of the pavement, which is at 4.2 miles. Continue another 0.6 mile to a gate. Open the gate and close it behind you, then drive another 0.4 mile to a fork. Park here unless you have a very rugged, high-clearance four-wheel-drive vehicle and the road is dry. Take the right fork and go 0.9 mile to a T. You will see an old metal bin on the left. Park here no matter what you are driving, and start walking.

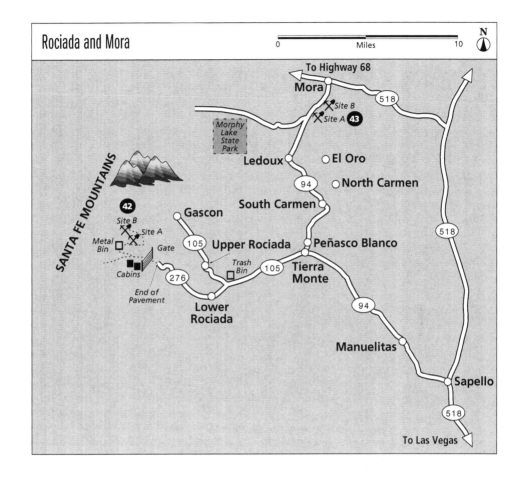

Go right at the T and hike 0.2 mile around an almost 180-degree curve. You will see an old mine structure and tailings on the left—this is site A. If you park at the fork, the hike to site A is a total of about 1.1 miles, all of it uphill. To get to site B, continue past site A for about another tenth of a mile. You will see a trail on the left, intersecting the road at about a 45-degree angle. Follow this up the hill for another 0.1 mile to site B. Alternatively, if you are up to it and have practice climbing on loose tailings, you can scramble straight up to site B from site A.

Rockhounding

Some of the nicest lepidolite we have ever found came from this location. At site A lots of small pieces of the material can be picked up. Some of this is finely grained and appropriate for cutting and polishing. Nice specimens of book lepidolite on white quartz can also be gathered, some of which are brightly colored.

At site B you will find large boulders of the material embedded in stark white quartz. Both fine- and coarse-grained specimens are present. Some of the ones we found are very bright pink and even red. It takes a lot of hard work to break the boulders and extract what you want, but it is definitely worth the effort. We also found garnet and green mica at both sites.

We made some very beautiful cabs by cutting the quartz-lepidolite rocks. The pink-white combination is very attractive. If you are up to the hike, this should be a must-go-to.

Mora

See map on page 73.

Land type: Mountainous forest.

GPS: Site A: N33° 57' 19"/ W105° 20' 31". Site B: N35° 57' 20"/W105° 20' 11".

Elevation: Site A: 8,996 feet. Site B: 7,459 feet.

Best time of year: May through October.

Material: Lepidolite, green mica, quartz, and unakite.

Tools: Geological hammer, small shovel, goggles, sledgehammer, chisels, gads, crowbar, and spray bottle.

Vehicle: Any.

Precautions and restrictions: Park well off the road. A large pull-off is found at site A, but there is only the shoulder at site B. Wear goggles if you decide to split the boulders.

Special attractions: At Fort Union National Monument, see a fort established in 1851 to help guard the Santa Fe Trail.

Finding the site: These road cuts are found about 3 miles southwest of Mora and about 20 miles northwest of Las Vegas. From Interstate 25, take Las Vegas exit 345 west. Turn right onto Business I-25 and drive a few hundred yards to Mills Road, then turn left (west) and drive another mile to Highway 518. Continue north to Sapello on Highway 518 past Storrie Lake and the dam, which is on the left (west), for a total of 11.6 miles. In Sapello, turn left (northwest) onto Highway 94 and continue another 16.9 miles. The road cut on the right is site A. Site B is another 0.2 mile at a road cut on the right.

From Mora at the junction of Highways 518 and 94, drive south on Highway 94 for 1.2 miles to site B on the left (east). Site A is another 0.2 mile on the left.

Rockhounding

At site A we found some very nice unakite. Look for the telltale green and orange/pink rocks. Unakite is the unofficial gemstone of the state of Virginia. It is a mixture of green epidote and orange/pink feldspar, and it makes some beautiful jewelry. More unakite can be picked up at site B. Some pieces are mixed with white and clear quartz, and they too cut into fine gemstones.

We also found some nice pieces of pink lepidote in white quartz here. A few big boulders with the mixture are located right below the road cut. If you have the energy, try to split these to see what treasures are inside. We also found green mica at both roadcuts.

Storrie Lake

Land type: High desert.
GPS: N35° 41' 27" / W105° 13' 45".
Elevation: 5,654 feet.
Best time of year: April through November.
Land manager: New Mexico Department of Transportation.
Material: Marine fossils.
Tools: Geological hammer, small chisel or screwdriver, and small shovel.
Vehicle: Any.
Precautions and restrictions: Park well off the road and beware of falling rocks.
Special attractions: Storrie Lake State Park has fishing, hiking, wildlife viewing, and camping. The Rough Rider Memorial collection at the City of Las Vegas Museum is great. The pools at Montezuma Hot Springs, located 6 miles northwest of Las Vegas on Highway 65, are free and the setting is beautiful.
Finding the site: This site is located just north of Las Vegas. From Interstate 25, take Las Vegas exit 345 west. Turn right onto Business I-25 and drive a few hundred yards to Mills Road, then turn left (west) and drive another mile to Highway 518. Continue north on Highway 518 for 5.7 miles past Storrie Lake and the dam, which is on the left (west). Park on the left (west) side of the road.

Rockhounding

The rocks in this area are full of marine fossils and make fine collection pieces. Pry the rocks open with a screwdriver or small chisel. The site we give is just one of many in the collecting area that continues for at least 5 miles north of the dam.

Sandia Crest

Land type: Mountainous forest.

GPS: N35° 10' 04" / W106° 21' 34".

Elevation: 4,860 feet.

Best time of year: April through October.

Land manager: New Mexico Department of Transportation.

Material: Crinoids, corals, brachiopods, bryozoans, and Pennsylvanian fossils.

Tools: Geological hammer and small shovel.

Vehicle: Any.

Precautions and restrictions: Highway 536 is very busy, but plenty of good pull-offs are available so there is no need to park in the road. Always be aware of the rocks above you when collecting in the road cut.

Special attractions: Wonder over miniature wood figures and more at the Tinkertown Museum in Sandia Park. The Museum of Archeological and Material Culture in Cedar Crest provides the timeline of the Sandia Mountains written in the rocks, water, and erosion. In Albuquerque you'll find the New Mexico

Sandia Crest fossils are close to Albuquerque.

Museum of Natural History and Science, a wonderful natural history museum with an emphasis on New Mexico, and the Maxwell Museum of Anthropology, which has exhibits reflecting the entire history of humankind, with an emphasis on the Southwest. Take a drive on the thrilling 65-mile Turquoise Trail, a National Scenic Byway.

Finding the site: This fossil area is located northeast of Albuquerque. From Albuquerque, drive east on Interstate 40 to exit 175 north (the Turquoise Trail). After exiting at the bottom of the ramp, go north on Highway 14. You will quickly come to the junction of Highways 14 and 333. Be sure to keep to the left and follow Highway 14, which goes under I-40. After passing under the interstate, drive another 5.9 miles. Turn left (northwest) onto Highway 536 toward Sandia Crest and drive 1.1 miles to a large road cut on the right (north). Park here.

Rockhounding

At this site we found crinoids, corals, and brachiopods. The GPS coordinates are for the first place we found fossils, but these oddities were also picked up at just about every road cut up the mountain. We did not make it to the summit, where bryozoans and Pennsylvanian fossils have been reported, as the area was snow-covered.

Madrid

Land type: High mesa desert.
GPS: N35° 23' 28" / W106° 09' 41".
Elevation: 6,206 feet.
Best time of year: March through October.
Land manager: New Mexico Department of Transportation.
Material: Anthracite, petrified wood, calcite crystals, and marine fossils.
Tools: Geological hammer and small shovel.
Vehicle: Any.
Precautions and restrictions: Park well off the road, as Highway 14 is a busy byway.
Special attractions: Wonder over miniature wood figures and more at the Tinkertown Museum in Sandia Park. The Museum of Archeological and Material Culture in Cedar Crest provides the timeline of the Sandia Mountains written in the rocks, water, and erosion. In Albuquerque you'll find the New Mexico Museum of Natural History and Science, a wonderful natural history museum with an emphasis on New Mexico, and the Maxwell Museum of Anthropology, which has exhibits reflecting the entire history of humankind, with an emphasis on the Southwest. Take a drive on the thrilling 65-mile Turquoise Trail, a National Scenic Byway.
Finding the site: Madrid is located about 40 miles northeast of Albuquerque. From Albuquerque, drive east on Interstate 40 to exit 175 north (the Turquoise Trail). After exiting at the bottom of the ramp, go north on Highway 14. You will quickly come to the junction of Highways 14 and 333. Be sure to keep to the left and follow Highway 14, which goes under I-40. After passing under the interstate, drive another 5.9 miles, which will take you past the Sandia Crest turnoff. Continue on Highway 14 another 21.8 miles (total of 27.7 miles on Highway 14), where you will see large coal mine tailings on the right (east) side of the road. Park at a pull-off on the right (east) side of the road.

Rockhounding

Anthracite is a very hard coal that takes a good polish and makes nice black gemstones. The hardest of the anthracite is called jet, and some of what we found here approached the jet category. As found they can also make handsome

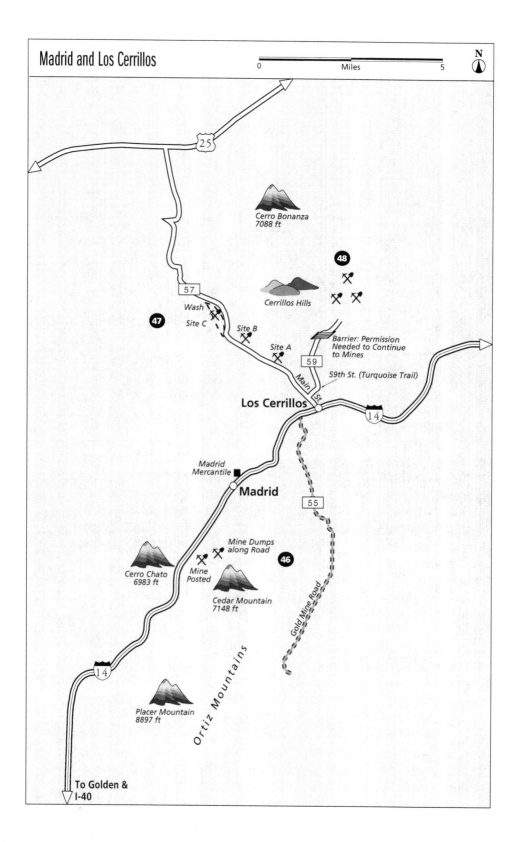

Madrid and Los Cerrillos

0 Miles 5

N

25

Cerro Bonanza
7088 ft

48

57

Cerrillos Hills

Wash

47

Site C

Site B

Site A

Barrier: Permission
Needed to Continue
to Mines

59

59th St. (Turquoise Trail)

Main St.

Los Cerrillos

14

Madrid
Mercantile

Madrid

55

Mine Dumps
along Road

46

Cerro Chato
6983 ft

Mine
Posted

Cedar Mountain
7148 ft

Gold Mine Road

Ortiz Mountains

14

Placer Mountain
8897 ft

**To Golden &
I-40**

display pieces, and are valuable additions to any collection. If you decide to polish some anthracite, be sure to wear adequate respiration equipment. Remember all the black lung disease in coal miners.

After you park, look for a dirt road to your south that heads toward the tailings piles. There are posted signs on both sides of the road, but enough samples of anthracite can be picked up off the road. We also found petrified wood, and others have reported calcite crystals and marine fossils.

Los Cerrillos Fossils

See map on page 80.

Land type: High desert.

GPS: Site A: N35° 47' 18"/ W106° 09' 21". Site B: N35° 27' 31"/ W106° 09' 23".

Elevation: Site A: 5,592 feet. Site B: 5,612 feet.

Best time of year: March through May and October through December.

Land manager: New Mexico Department of Transportation.

Material: Marine fossils and calcite.

Tools: Geological hammer.

Vehicle: Any.

Precautions and restrictions: There is some private land in the area, so be sure not to trespass. Park well off the road at all three sites.

Special attractions: Wonder over miniature wood figures and more at the Tinkertown Museum in Sandia Park. The Museum of Archeological and Material Culture in Cedar Crest provides the timeline of the Sandia Mountains written in the rocks, water, and erosion. In Albuquerque you'll find the New Mexico Museum of Natural History and Science and the Maxwell Museum of Anthropology, which has exhibits reflecting the entire history of humankind, with an emphasis on the Southwest. Take a drive on the thrilling 65-mile Turquoise Trail, a National Scenic Byway.

Finding the site: This fossil area is located west of Los Cerrillos and east of Interstate 25. From Madrid Mercantile in Madrid, drive 2.7 miles on Highway 14 to Los Cerrillos. At the junction of Highway 14 and County Road 57 (Main Street), go west on CR 57 for 0.3 mile to where the road turns north and then turns west again immediately after crossing the railroad tracks. Continue on CR 57 for 2.3 miles and you will see a dirt road heading off to the north on the right. Park here for site A. Site B is another 0.3 mile. There is no place to park at this road cut, so drive another 200 feet to a pull-off on the left and walk back. To get to site C, turn right in another 0.7 mile and park off a sandy road. If you are coming from the north, take I-25 to exit 267 and drive 4.4 miles on CR 57 to site C.

Rockhounding

Site A has marine fossils in the loose rock around the road cut. The best site at this location is B, which has numerous marine fossils in the rocks. Site C is a wash, and more fossils can be found in the rocks. In addition, a green limestone that contains similar critters can be cut and polished.

Los Cerrillos Turquoise

See map on page 80.
Land type: High desert.
Best time of year: March through November.
Land manager: Cerrillos Hills Historic Park.
Material: Turquoise.
Tools: None.
Vehicle: Any.
Precautions and restrictions: No collecting allowed.
Special attractions: Be sure to stop and walk around the ghost town of Madrid.
Finding the site: Cerrillos Hills Historic Park is located north of town, and access is available through the village of Cerrillos. The hills are generally bounded by County Road 57 on the south and west, Interstate 25 on the northwest, and Highway 14 (the Turquoise Trail Scenic Byway) on the south and east. To get there from Madrid Mercantile in Madrid, go 2.7 miles on Highway 14 to County Road 57 (Main Street) and turn left (west). Drive 0.3 mile, turn right (north), and cross the railroad tracks. Continue straight ahead; the road becomes 59th Street. At 0.6 mile bear left, continuing on 59th Street. This is the historic Turquoise Trail. Continue 1.3 miles to a barrier. You can park here, but to continue on to the mines you need permission.

Rockhounding

As you hike or bike along the trails in the Cerrillos Hills Historic Park, evidence of many of the old mines is apparent. Prehistoric stone rings and petroglyphs from ancient Native American days can also be seen.

Galisteo

Land type: High desert.
GPS: N35° 26' 42" / W105° 55' 04".
Elevation: 6,327 feet.
Best time of year: March through November.
Land manager: New Mexico Department of Transportation.
Material: Petrified wood, agate, and jasper.
Tools: Geological hammer, spray bottle, and small shovel.
Vehicle: Any.
Precautions and restrictions: Park well off the road and respect private property.
Special attractions: Santa Fe has several wonderful museums, including the Institute of American Indian Arts and the Museum of International Folk Art.
Finding the site: This site is located south of Santa Fe. From Santa Fe, drive northeast on Interstate 25 to exit 290 (Clines Corner exit) and go south on U.S. Highway 285 for 6.6 miles. Turn right (southwest) onto Highway 41, follow it 1.6 miles, and park on either side of the road.

Rockhounding

Though jasper is reported in this area, we found none. We made a number of stops all the way past Galisteo without results. But what we did find was very exciting: some very colorful and cuttable petrified wood. The GPS coordinates are for the spot described in the directions, where we found this material on the west (right) side of the road. You may want to try stopping at a number of other areas within a mile before or after the main site. We also found agates in the area.

Unfortunately, by the time this book is published, the wood will probably be depleted, but some will always be eroding out of the topsoil. This area appears to rapidly developing. We confined our searching to the right-of-way, but if you can get permission, a lot of very colorful petrified wood might be found in the low hills surrounding the main road.

Laguna de Perro

Land type: High desert.
GPS: N34° 34' 37" / W105° 57' 54".
Elevation: 6,059 feet.
Best time of year: March through May, October, and November.
Land manager: New Mexico Department of Transportation.
Material: Halite.
Tools: Geological hammer, small shovel, and soft packaging material.
Vehicle: Any.
Precautions and restrictions: Park well off U.S. Highway 60, as it can be very busy.
Special attractions: View the Abó, Gran Quivira, and Quarai ruins at Salinas Pueblo Missions National Monument in Mountainair.
Finding the site: This area is located just east of the town of Willard. Take Interstate 25 to exit 175 east, which is the US 60 exit. Drive east on US 60 for

The halite at Laguna de Perro is beautiful but fragile.

2.1 miles, at which point you will cross the Rio Grande. Continue a total of 50 miles on US 60 to its junction with Highway 42 in the town of Willard. From the junction, continue east on US 60 for 4 more miles to a salt lake on the left (north) side of the road. A good pull-off can be found on the right (south) side.

Rockhounding

Some nice examples of halite crystals can be found here, most of which have been formed around vegetation. They can be difficult to collect and get home, as they are very fragile. Be prepared with some very soft packaging material. Even if the specimens make it to your display case intact, some will eventually fall apart.

Sumner Lake

Land type: High desert.

GPS: N34° 37' 31" / W104° 26' 42".

Elevation: 4,416 feet.

Best time of year: March through November.

Land manager: New Mexico Department of Transportation.

Material: Agate, petrified wood, jasper, feldspar, and quartzite.

Tools: Geological hammer and small shovel.

Vehicle: Any.

Precautions and restrictions: Park well off the road and respect private and park lands.

Special Attractions: There is good fishing in Sumner Lake. Fort Sumner is a walk through history; among its attractions are the Old Fort Sumner Museum and Fort Sumner State Monument.

Finding the site: From the junction of U.S. Highways 60 and 84 in Fort Sumner, drive northwest on US 84 for 9.9 miles. Turn west onto Highway 203 toward Sumner Lake State Park. After 5.3 miles you will enter the park, at which point you continue another 0.9 mile to the dam. From the dam it is 1.4 miles to the main campground turnoff. Turn left at this point and continue on Highway 203. You are now out of the park and at the beginning of the collecting area.

Rockhounding

The GPS coordinates were taken 2.8 miles from the turn after the main campground. We found agate, petrified wood, jasper, feldspar, and quartzite at this stop, as well as every other place we looked. Nothing was abundant anywhere, but with diligence a nice bag of pretty tumblers can be gathered. We found a few pieces of pink feldspar that were rather solid. They worked up into nice moonstone-like gems. The quartzite pieces are quite colorful and tumble nicely.

There is a lot of private land in the area and it appears quite a bit of development is taking place, so without permission, rockhounds have to stick to the right-of-way. Petrified wood is abundant around the dam; however, all you can do is look at it because this area is in the state park and collecting is illegal there.

Santa Rosa

Land type: High desert.
GPS: Site A: N34° 57' 16" / W104° 36' 38". Site B: N34° 57' 17" / W104° 36' 12".
Elevation: Site A: 4,875 feet. Site B: 4,950 feet.
Best time of year: March through November.
Land manager: New Mexico Department of Transportation.
Material: Marine fossils, agate, quartzite, petrified wood, feldspar, calcite, and swirled limestone.
Tools: Geological hammer and small shovel. If you intend to get large chunks of the swirled limestone, you'll need a large pick.
Vehicle: Any.
Precautions and restrictions: Highway 156 can be busy, so be sure to park well off the pavement. Be careful of loose rocks above you. If you chisel, please wear goggles.
Special attractions: Santa Rosa is known as the City of Natural Lakes, and opportunities for fishing and other water sports abound.
Finding the site: This site is located several miles east of Santa Rosa. Take exit 277 off Interstate 40 and go south on U.S. Highway 84, but then quickly turn left (east) onto Highway 156. Drive 1.9 miles to site A, where a good pull-off can be found on the left (north) side of the road. Continue on Highway 156 another 0.4 mile to site B and park on the right (south), just before the road cut.

Rockhounding

At site A we found fossils, agate, quartzite, petrified wood, and feldspar. The agate tends to be white and in small pieces. Some of the quartzite is colorful, and the petrified wood is well formed.

The swirled limestone and more marine fossils were found at site B. The limestone is available in shades of white, cream, brown, yellow, and orange. The colors are all swirled together, and the material polishes well. Calcite was found at all sites.

Southeastern New Mexico

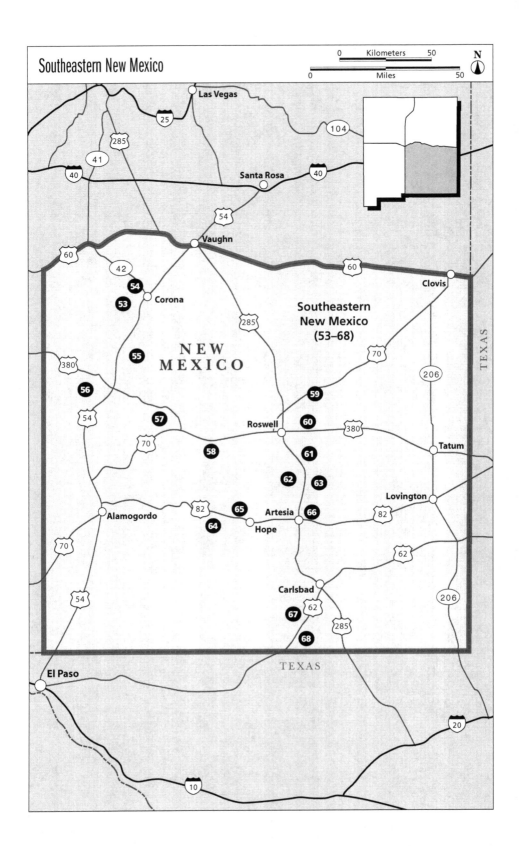

Southeastern New Mexico

Southeastern
New Mexico
(53–68)

Red Cloud Mines

Land type: Mountainous forest.

GPS: N34° 11' 49" / W105° 44' 24".

Elevation: 7,386 feet.

Best time of year: May through October.

Land manager: Cibola National Forest.

Material: Fluorite, wulfenite, barite, chalcopyrite, chrysacolla, chalcocite, malachite, azurite, bastnaesite, cerussite, sphalerite, galena, vanadinite, goethite, and hematite pseudomorphs after pyrite.

Tools: Geological hammer, large pick, spray bottle, very soft wrapping material, chisels, sledgehammer, goggles, gads, and small shovel.

Vehicle: Any vehicle is OK most of the time, but if there has been a lot of rain or if the snow is melting, four-wheel drive is needed.

Precautions and restrictions: The fluorite mine has a lot of loose rocks above, so be very careful if you are digging or chiseling in this area. Always wear goggles when hammering. This is bear and cougar country, so take the proper precautions.

Special attractions: The Salinas Pueblo Missions National Monument in Mountainair and the Wildland Firefighters Museum in Capitan are both worth a visit. A nice Forest Service campground is located near the mines.

Finding the site: These mines are located southwest of Corona. From Corona, take U.S. Highway 54 southwest for 4 miles to County Road A027 (Forest Road 144). Turn right (west) and follow this road for 3.1 miles to where it ends at Forest Road 104. Turn left (south) and continue 2.7 miles to Forest Road 99 (County Road A023). Turn right (west) and drive 3.4 miles, at which point you will see the fluorite mine on the right (north) and the copper mine on the left (south). Park on either side.

If coming from the south from Carrizozo, drive north on US 54 for 36.9 miles and turn left (west) onto Forest Road 161 (County Road A019). Drive 1.3 miles and turn right (north) onto FR 104. Continue for 2.1 miles to FR 99 (CR A023), then turn left (west) and drive 3.4 miles to the mines.

Rockhounding

There is a great variety of minerals at this site. We found fluorite, wulfenite, barite, chalcopyrite, chrysacolla, chalcocite, malachite, and azurite, while others

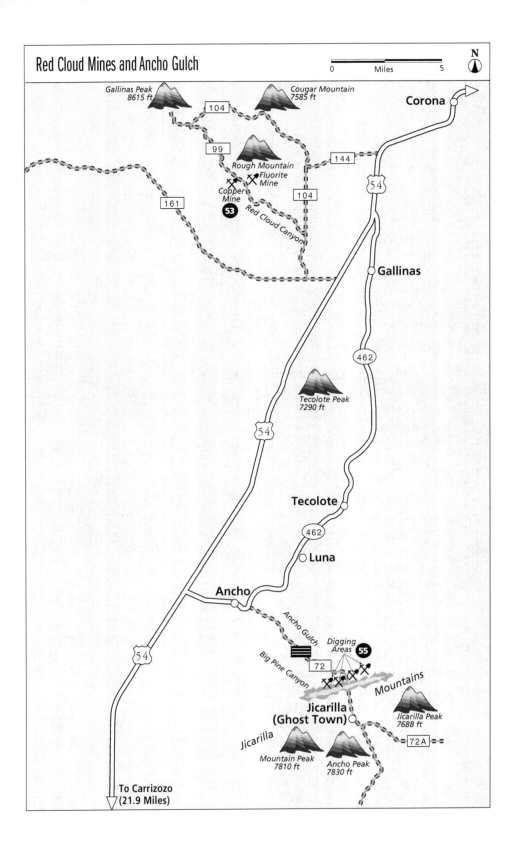

Red Cloud Mines and Ancho Gulch

The Red Cloud fluorite mine is a must for the serious rockhound.

have reported bastnaesite, cerussite, sphalerite, galena, vanadinite, goethite, and hematite pseudomorphs after pyrite. When we were there, the property did not appear to be posted.

This is a must-go-to for any serious mineral collector. The fluorite cubes are opaque but bright purple. We found some chocolate-colored wulfenite, but it is extremely fragile and special handling is absolutely necessary. The copper ores are very bright, and some are solid enough to cut and polish.

The fluorite mine looks like a quarry and is easy to see, while the tailings from the copper mine are partially grown over. Careful observation will reveal the telltale colors of copper ore. It pays to dig where you see color. Don't take too much from this location—please save some for us!

Highway 42 Crystals

Land type: Forested high desert.

GPS: N34° 16' 22" / W105° 36' 48".

Elevation: 6,234 feet.

Best time of year: March through October.

Land manager: New Mexico Department of Transportation.

Material: Calcite crystals, quartz crystals, and zeolites.

Tools: Geological hammer, crowbar, sledgehammer, chisel, gads, and goggles.

Vehicle: Any.

Precautions and restrictions: Folks drive fast on Highway 42, so park well off it. Be careful of loose rocks above you in the road cut. Always wear goggles when chiseling.

Special attractions: The Salinas Pueblo Missions National Monument in Mountainair and the Wildland Firefighters Museum in Capitan are both worth a visit.

Finding the site: This site is located just a bit northwest of the town of Corona. From the junction of U.S. Highway 60 and Highway 42 in Willard, drive southeast on Highway 42 for 33.8 miles to a large road cut. A good pull-off can be found just south of the road cut on the right (west) side of the road. From Corona, the site can be reached by driving northwest on Highway 42 for 1.8 miles.

Rockhounding

The basalt in this road cut is full of crystal pockets. Nicely formed calcite crystals and druzy quartz are quite common. We found the zeolites to be a bit scarce, but they can be located with careful observation. Removing these pockets takes effort and persistence; however, they can make beautiful display pieces and are well worth the effort.

Ancho Gulch

See map on page 92.
Land type: Hilly, forested high desert.
GPS: N33° 52' 15" / W105° 39' 50".
Elevation: 7,010 feet.
Best time of year: April through October.
Land manager: Lincoln National Forest.
Material: Auriferous pyrite, quartz, native gold, hematite, and suspect silver (argentiferous galena).
Tools: Geological hammer, small shovel, and a substantial pocket knife.
Vehicle: Any.
Precautions and restrictions: Be sure to park off the road, and do not trespass in the ghost town.
Special attractions: The ghost town of Jicarilla can be observed from your vehicle; you are not allowed to walk around the town. The Salinas Pueblo Missions National Monument in Mountainair and the Wildland Firefighters Museum in Capitan are both worth a visit. There is a nice Forest Service campground right before the mines.
Finding the site: These mines are located northeast of Carrizozo. From the junction of U.S. Highways 380 and 54 in Carrizozo, drive north 21.9 miles on US 54. Turn right (east) onto Highway 462 and travel 2.4 miles to the small community of Ancho. After another 0.2 mile, turn right and cross over the railroad tracks. Drive another 3.6 miles, cross the cattle guard, and enter the national forest. You will now be on Forest Road 72 heading south. Continue another 3.4 miles, crossing Ancho Gulch, then immediately turn right (west) and park.

Rockhounding

While looking for the tailings of the mines around the ghost town of Jicarilla, we discovered this location. The town itself has been posted by the Forest Service, probably in an attempt to control vandalism. However, Ancho Gulch seems to contain many of the minerals reported from the dump sites. Much of the quartz appears to contain pyrite cubes, and many of these are auriferous, meaning that they contain gold. You can tell which ones have some of the precious metal by sticking them with the point of your pocket knife or some similarly

Gold can be found near the ghost town of Jicarilla.

sharp object. If it has gold in it, the point will sink in, since it is obviously softer than other pyrite.

The native gold is very small, and you really need a loupe to look through to be sure. This also seems to just smear when stuck with a sharp point. The hematite is found in black masses up to 2 inches across. You can scratch it with a piece of quartz, and if the powder is reddish, it is probably hematite. The silver scratches a white powder.

Valley of Fires State Recreation Area

Land type: High desert covered by volcanic lava-flow beds.
Best time of year: All year.
Land manager: New Mexico State Parks.
Material: Volcanic lava flows.
Tools: None.
Vehicle: Any.
Precautions and restrictions: No collecting allowed in the recreation area. When snakes first appear in the spring, they like to lie around on the warm black rocks, so take the proper precautions.
Special attractions: The Three Rivers Petroglyph Site, located 28 miles south of Carrizozo off Highway 54, contains more than 20,000 pieces of ancient graffiti. Contact the BLM's Las Cruces District Office for more information (see appendix B).
Finding the site: From Carrizozo, take U.S. Highway 380 west 4 miles to the entrance of the recreation area on the left (south). This is a fee area.

Rockhounding

This is an area of relatively recent lava flows, and the contortions and contusions of the landscape are incredible. It is a good place to stop and have a picnic lunch while on the way to a collection site. The area consists of hundreds of acres of distorted, twisted lava. Some of it is almost 200 feet thick, and the region runs for nearly 50 miles. Several volcanoes were responsible for this deposit. One vent, Little Black, is located a few miles north of the town of Carrizozo.

Lincoln County

Land type: Mountainous forest.
GPS: N33° 32' 38" / W105° 33' 20".
Elevation: 5,320 feet.
Best time of year: April through October.
Land manager: New Mexico Department of Transportation.
Material: Marine fossils, calcite, and green limestone.
Tools: Geological hammer and small shovel.
Vehicle: Any.
Precautions and restrictions: U.S. Highway 380 is a busy, winding road with only a few places to pull off, so be very careful parking. While searching around, lots of loose rocks will be above you. It might be advisable to wear a hard hat and goggles.
Special attractions: The Salinas Pueblo Missions National Monument in Mountainair and the Wildland Firefighters Museum in Capitan are both worth a visit.
Finding the site: From the post office in Capitan, drive east on US 380 for 1.2 miles. A good turnoff is located on the left (north) side of the road. Park here.

Rockhounding

This is just one of the locations along this stretch of road where we found fossils. Just about all the road cuts between Capitan and Lincoln contain these oddities. Most are deformed, but a few show their original shape. We also found green limestone here. It is a pale apple green, polishes well, and works up into some very pretty pieces.

Picacho

Land type: High desert.

GPS: N33° 20' 22" / W105° 02' 43".

Elevation: 4,956 feet.

Best time of year: March through November.

Land manager: New Mexico Department of Transportation.

Material: Marine fossils, calcite crystals, quartz crystals, and zeolites.

Tools: Geological hammer, goggles, sledgehammer, chisel, gads, and small shovel.

Vehicle: Any.

Precautions and restrictions: This is a very busy road, so park well off the pavement. Be careful of loose rocks above you, and always wear goggles when chiseling.

Special attractions: The Wildland Firefighters Museum in Capitan is well worth a visit. Bottomless Lakes State Park outside Roswell offers trout fishing, camping, hiking, and geological exploration. Meet little alien folk at Roswell's International UFO Museum & Research Center.

Finding the site: This area is west of Roswell along U.S. Highway 70. From the west end of Roswell at the junction of the U.S. Highway 285 Bypass and US 70, drive 27.8 miles to a large road cut on the left (south) and park.

Rockhounding

We found lots of fossils in the loose rocks in this area. Most are quite deformed, but they make interesting specimens. Many of the molds are filled with both calcium and quartz crystals, and if they can be extracted without shattering, would make handsome display pieces. A few of the cavities contain various zeolites.

Roswell Pecos Diamonds

Land type: Desert.
GPS: N33° 36' 26" / W104° 19' 58".
Elevation: 3,639 feet.
Best time of year: October through May.
Land manager: Bureau of Land Management, Pecos District.
Material: Pecos diamonds and petrified wood.
Tools: Geological hammer and small shovel.
Vehicle: Any vehicle is fine up to the last turn, after which a high-clearance four-wheel drive is needed.
Precautions and restrictions: You will be walking through some vegetation—think *snakes* during warm weather.
Special attractions: The Wildland Firefighters Museum in Capitan is well worth a visit. Bottomless Lakes State Park outside Roswell offers trout fishing, camping, hiking, and geological exploration. Meet little alien folk at Roswell's International UFO Museum & Research Center. The Dexter National Fish Hatchery is the only hatchery dedicated to the preservation of endangered desert fish species.
Finding the site: This prolific area is located about 15 miles northeast of Roswell. From downtown Roswell at the junction of U.S. Highway 380 (Second Street) and U.S. Highway 285 (Main Street), drive north on US 285 for 5.2 miles. Turn right (northeast) onto U.S. Highway 70, continue 11 miles, and cross the Pecos River. Drive another 2.4 miles and cross Bob Crosby draw. Continue another 0.7 mile and turn left onto County Road 1 (there is an old stone school house on the left before the turn). Immediately after you turn you will see a sign on the left that reads WOOTON BOSQUE GRANDE. Drive 0.4 mile and take the second left (west). Park here, or if you have a high-clearance four-wheel-drive vehicle, you can continue on for another 0.4 mile to where the road ends. Whether you walk or drive, follow this road to a circle at the end. There is an old oil tank situated to the west about a quarter mile in the distance. Work your way toward the land around that structure.

Rockhounding

This is just one of the many areas near Roswell where rockhounds can pick up some fine Pecos diamonds. If you walk the road, a few of the gems will be seen

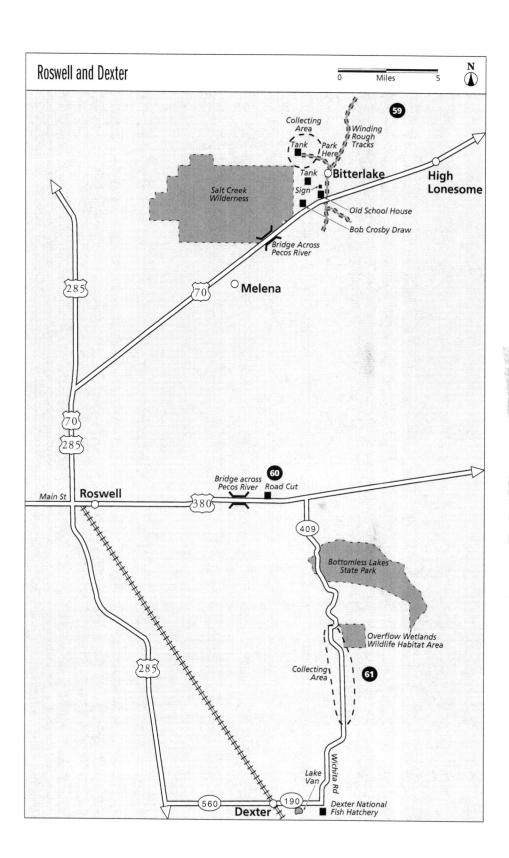

after about an eighth of a mile. Upon reaching the circle, work your way toward the structure and be on the lookout for more diamonds. If you find one, carefully search the immediate area. One has to be quite observant to spot the little critters. Around the structure, look over any disturbed ground.

The diamonds found here are both the standard double-terminated type as well as the clustered multipoint sort. The latter make beautiful pendants, while the former are great for rings and earrings.

Besides this particular site, spend some time driving and walking around the area—you may find your very own Pecos diamond hot spot. These gems are spread over a very wide area, so take some time to explore—and leave a few for us.

Roswell Selenite

See map on page 101.
Land type: Desert.
GPS: N33° 23' 47" / W104° 22' 45".
Elevation: 3,674 feet.
Best time of year: October through May.
Land manager: New Mexico Department of Transportation.
Material: Selenite.
Tools: Geological hammer, shovel, pick, and crowbar if you want large chunks.
Vehicle: Any.
Precautions and restrictions: This site is located on a very busy road, so park appropriately. Watch for the rocks above you, as they are soft and often fall.
Special attractions: The Wildland Firefighters Museum in Capitan is well worth a visit. Bottomless Lakes State Park outside Roswell offers trout fishing, camping, hiking, and geological exploration. Meet little alien folk at Roswell's International UFO Museum & Research Center. The Dexter National Fish Hatchery is the only hatchery dedicated to the preservation of endangered desert fish species.
Finding the site: This area is located on U.S. Highway 380 about 7 miles east of Roswell. From downtown Roswell at the junction of Main Street (U.S. Highway 285) and US 380, drive east on US 380 for 6.2 miles. Cross the Pecos River and continue another mile up the hill to a large road cut. Park here.

Rockhounding

Selenite of every possible type can be found here: nice clear pieces as well as pure white, orange, black, brown, and every combination of the above. Some large pieces for carving can also be pried out of this road cut.

Dexter

See map on page 101.
Land type: Desert.
GPS: N33° 14' 08" / W104° 19' 42".
Elevation: 3,450 feet.
Best time of year: October through May.
Land manager: New Mexico Department of Transportation.
Material: Selenite, petrified wood, agate, carnelian, and Pecos diamonds.
Tools: Geological hammer, small shovel, and soft wrapping material.
Vehicle: Any.
Precautions and restrictions: Park well off the road. Think *snake* when it is warm.
Special attractions: The Wildland Firefighters Museum in Capitan is well worth a visit. Bottomless Lakes State Park outside Roswell offers trout fishing, camping, hiking, and geological exploration. Meet little alien folk at Roswell's International UFO Museum & Research Center. The Dexter National Fish Hatchery is the only hatchery dedicated to the preservation of endangered desert fish species.
Finding the site: This area is located a few miles northeast of Dexter. From the junction of Highways 2 and 190 in Dexter, drive 2.1 miles east on Highway 190 past Lake Van and the Dexter National Fish Hatchery. Turn left (north) onto Wichita Road (County Road 1) and continue 4.9 miles. Pull off the road here. The collecting area extends quite a ways toward Bottomless Lakes State Park.

Rockhounding

We found just a few Pecos diamonds at this location—in about fifteen minutes of looking, we picked up only three. They were not the standard double terminators but florets with many points. All forms of selenite can be found here. Some of these have nicely formed blades, but they are very fragile. If you intend to get them home intact, you'd better bring some soft wrapping material and handle them very carefully. In some of the pieces of selenite, you will see tiny double-terminated Pecos diamonds. These pieces would make wonderful micromounts. We also found a few small pieces of petrified wood and agate at the site.

Rio Felix

Land type: Desert and agricultural.

GPS: N33° 05' 49" / W104° 26' 32".

Elevation: 3,611 feet.

Best time of year: October through April.

Land manager: New Mexico Department of Transportation.

Material: Agate, jasper, and petrified wood.

Tools: Geological hammer, small shovel, and spray bottle.

Vehicle: Any.

Precautions and restrictions: The rest area is located along a very busy road, so be sure to park well off the pavement.

Special attractions: Read the placard in the rest area. The history of this region is very interesting. Bottomless Lakes State Park outside Roswell offers trout fishing, camping, hiking, and geological exploration. Meet little alien folk at Roswell's International UFO Museum & Research Center. The Dexter National Fish Hatchery is the only hatchery dedicated to the preservation of endangered desert fish species.

Finding the site: This site is about 20 miles south of Roswell. From the west side of Roswell at the junction of U.S. Highway 70 and the U.S. Highway 285 Bypass, travel 7.9 miles south on the bypass. At this point the road joins with US 285. Continue another 17.4 miles to a rest area on the right (west), immediately after crossing the Rio Felix. Park here.

Rockhounding

Just walking around the rest area, we found a number of small pieces of agate, jasper, and petrified wood, some of which were very colorful. None were large enough to cut but would make nice tumblers. It appears that most of the land in the area is private, but the right-of-way is quite large, offering adequate opportunity for rockhounds.

East of Hagerman

Land type: Desert and agricultural.
GPS: N33° 06' 25" / W104° 16' 11".
Elevation: 3,424 feet.
Best time of year: October through May.
Land manager: New Mexico Department of Transportation.
Material: Petrified wood, agate, and Pecos diamonds.
Tools: Geological hammer and small shovel.
Vehicle: Any.
Precautions and restrictions: Park well off the road and respect private land.
Special attractions: Bottomless Lakes State Park outside Roswell offers trout fishing, camping, hiking, and geological exploration. Meet little alien folk at Roswell's International UFO Museum & Research Center. The Dexter National Fish Hatchery is the only hatchery dedicated to the preservation of endangered desert fish species.
Finding the site: This area is about 5 miles east of Hagerman. From the junction of Highways 2 and 249 on the western outskirts of Hagerman, drive east on Highway 249 for 3.4 miles to the bridge over the Pecos River. (Follow the signs carefully for Highway 249 because the road twists and turns.) Continue over the bridge and go another 1.6 miles. Park on the right (west) side of the road.

Rockhounding

We went to this location to find Pecos diamonds, but instead picked up a number of nice but small pieces of agate and petrified wood. The wood is rather colorful and tumbles nicely. While we did not find any diamonds, many people have reported that they are in the area. Our experience has taught us that when hunting for Pecos diamonds, you have to cover a bit of ground. They could be abundant in one spot but absent 100 feet farther on, so just because we didn't find any doesn't mean that you won't.

Much of the land off the right-of-way is private, so stick to the road or get permission.

West of Hope

Land type: Rolling grassy hills.
GPS: N32° 52' 08" / W105° 00' 24" (beginning of road to quarry).
Elevation: 2,923 feet.
Best time of year: March through November.
Land manager: Bureau of Land Management, Pecos District.
Material: Permian marine fossils in limestone.
Tools: Geological hammer, gads, picks, sledgehammer, chisels, and goggles.
Vehicle: Four-wheel drive (or walking) is advised for Helena Road.
Special attractions: Near Carlsbad you'll find Living Desert State Park, which features an interpretive center for Chihuahuan Desert flora, fauna, and geology, and Carlsbad Caverns National Park (see site 67). Across the border in Texas is Guadalupe Mountains National Park, where you can enjoy camping, hiking, backpacking, wildlife viewing, birding, nature photography, stargazing, and horseback riding. The rest area on the south side of U.S. Highway 180/62 just west of the Texas–New Mexico line has a wonderful educational exhibit on the geology, history, and legends of the area. In addition, the drive from the junction of US 180/62 with Texas Highway 54 to Whites City presents spectacular views of the jagged mountains within Guadalupe National Park. The drive west from this site along U.S. Highway 82 through Cloudcroft and down into Alamagordo climbs to about 8,000 feet and provides some incredible vistas of the geological forces that formed this area. Be prepared for cold, snow, and slippery roads if driving here in winter.
Finding the site: From Artesia, drive west on US 82 to its junction with Highway 13 west of Hope. Continue west on US 82 for 4.3 miles, then turn left (south) onto Helena Road and continue 1 mile to quarry on the left. Helena Road may require four-wheel drive.

Rockhounding

We didn't drive down to the quarry itself because it was snowing heavily at the time we visited (in February), but we could see it from US 82. It has been reported that the marine fossils are better formed here than those in the road cuts on US 82. They do, however, require extensive hard work and tools to extract.

U.S. Highway 82 Road Cut Fossils

Land type: Rolling grassy hills.
GPS: N35° 53' 02" / W104° 19' 05".
Elevation: 4,708 feet.
Best time of year: March through November.
Land manager: New Mexico Department of Transportation.
Material: Permian marine fossils in limestone.
Tools: Geological hammer, gads, picks, sledgehammer, chisels, and goggles.
Vehicle: Any.
Special attractions: Near Carlsbad you'll find Living Desert State Park, which features an interpretive center for Chihuahuan Desert flora, fauna, and geology, and Carlsbad Caverns National Park (see site 67). Across the border in Texas is Guadalupe Mountains National Park, where you can enjoy camping, hiking, backpacking, wildlife viewing, birding, nature photography, stargazing, and horseback riding. The rest area on the south side of U.S. Highway 180/62 just west of the Texas–New Mexico line has a wonderful educational exhibit on the geology, history, and legends of the area. In addition, the drive from the junction of US 180/62 with Texas Highway 54 to Whites City presents spectacular views of the jagged mountains within Guadalupe National Park. The drive west from this site along U.S. Highway 82 through Cloudcroft and down into Alamagordo climbs to about 8,000 feet and provides some incredible vistas of the geological forces that formed this area. Be prepared for cold, snow, and slippery roads if driving here in winter.
Finding the site: From Artesia, drive west on US 82 to its junction with Highway 13. Continue west on US 82 for 0.1 mile to a road cut that has fossils imbedded in the limestone. Continue stopping at road cuts for the next several miles.

Rockhounding

There are a variety of marine fossils embedded in the limestone, but many are deformed and hard to recognize. Removing them requires quite a bit of effort using hammers and chisels. It takes a bit of work to find some good specimens, but it's well worth the time.

Artesia

Land type: Flat high desert.
GPS: N29° 17' 59" / W103° 38' 32".
Elevation: 2,794 feet.
Best time of year: October through April.
Land manager: Bureau of Land Management, Pecos District.
Material: Pecos diamonds, selenite, limb casts, banded agate, moss agate, jasper, and quartz crystals.
Tools: Small shovel, geological hammer, and spray bottle.
Vehicle: Any.
Special attractions: Near Carlsbad you'll find Living Desert State Park, which features an interpretive center for Chihuahuan Desert flora, fauna, and geology, and Carlsbad Caverns National Park (see site 67). Across the border in Texas is Guadalupe Mountains National Park, where you can enjoy camping, hiking, backpacking, wildlife viewing, birding, nature photography, stargazing, and horseback riding. The rest area on the south side of U.S. Highway 180/62 just west of the Texas–New Mexico line has a wonderful educational exhibit on the geology, history, and legends of the area. In addition, the drive from the junction of US 180/62 with Texas Highway 54 to Whites City presents spectacular views of the jagged mountains within Guadalupe National Park. The drive west from this site along U.S. Highway 82 through Cloudcroft and down into Alamagordo climbs to about 8,000 feet and provides some incredible vistas of the geological forces that formed this area. Be prepared for cold, snow, and slippery roads if driving here in winter.
Finding the site: This collecting area is along the banks of the Pecos River, both north and south. At the junction of U.S. Highways 285 and 82 in Artesia, drive east on US 82. After crossing the Pecos River, take the first road left (north), which is County Road 200 (Karr Ranch Road), or south (right), County Road 201 (Chalk Bluff Road). The collecting area is on both sides of these roads for many miles.

Rockhounding

This area contains a variety of material. Drive along the county roads, stopping periodically to search both sides. We found nice small pieces of colorful agate and jasper, excellent for tumbling. Some red moss agate pieces were large enough to slice. We also found selenite and limb casts, and others have reported quartz crystals.

Pecos diamonds are scattered throughout the area. They are sometimes difficult to locate because they resemble the color of the desert floor, and one often has to get down on all fours on the sandy ground to identify them. Walk slowly and stop often to search the immediate area around you. We have also had good luck finding these little gems in areas around large ant hills where the ground has been disturbed by the working of the ants. They range from $\frac{1}{16}$ inch to 1 inch. After a half hour of collecting, we found about a dozen Pecos diamonds at the William S. Huey Wildlife Area sign, 3.4 miles north on CR 200.

Carlsbad Caverns National Park

Land type: Caverns located under high-desert hills.
Best time of year: All year.
Land manager: Carlsbad Caverns National Park.
Tools: None.
Vehicle: Any.
Precautions and restrictions: No collecting allowed.
Finding the site: From Carlsbad, take U.S. Highway 62/180 south for about 23 miles to Whites City. Turn right (west) at the Carlsbad Access Road and drive 7 miles to the visitor center. From El Paso, Texas, take US 62/180 north for about 150 miles to Whites City. Turn left (west) at the Carlsbad Access Road and drive 7 miles to the visitor center.

Rockhounding

One hundred thirteen caves, formed by the sulfuric acid dissolution of limestone, are found in this park. The primary attraction is the tour of the main cavern.

Eddy County

Land type: Rolling high-desert hills.
GPS: N32° 01' 45" / W32° 02' 55".
Elevation: 3,450 feet.
Best time of year: All year.
Land manager: New Mexico Department of Transportation.
Material: Layered marble.
Tools: Geological hammer, sledgehammer, chisels, gads, crowbar, and goggles.
Vehicle: Any.
Special attractions: Near Carlsbad you'll find Living Desert State Park, which features an interpretive center for Chihuahuan Desert flora, fauna, and geology, and Carlsbad Caverns National Park (see site 67). Across the border in Texas is Guadalupe Mountains National Park, where you can enjoy camping, hiking, backpacking, wildlife viewing, birding, nature photography, stargazing, and horseback riding. The rest area on the south side of U.S. Highway 180/62 just west of the Texas–New Mexico line has a wonderful educational exhibit on the geology, history, and legends of the area. In addition, the drive from the junction of US 180/62 with Texas Highway 54 to Whites City presents spectacular views of the jagged mountains within Guadalupe National Park.
Finding the site: Collecting is along road cuts on US 180/62 between the Texas–New Mexico state line and Whites City. We found a plentiful location 4.5 miles northeast of the state line on both sides of the road.

Rockhounding

This location has a very interesting layered marble of basically three colors: black, white, and gray. It is plentiful in some road cuts and is good carving material. The marble can also make nice adornment for a rock garden or small garden pool. When collecting, look for areas of new road work in particular. The road cut we found was one where road work was being done at the time.

Southwestern New Mexico

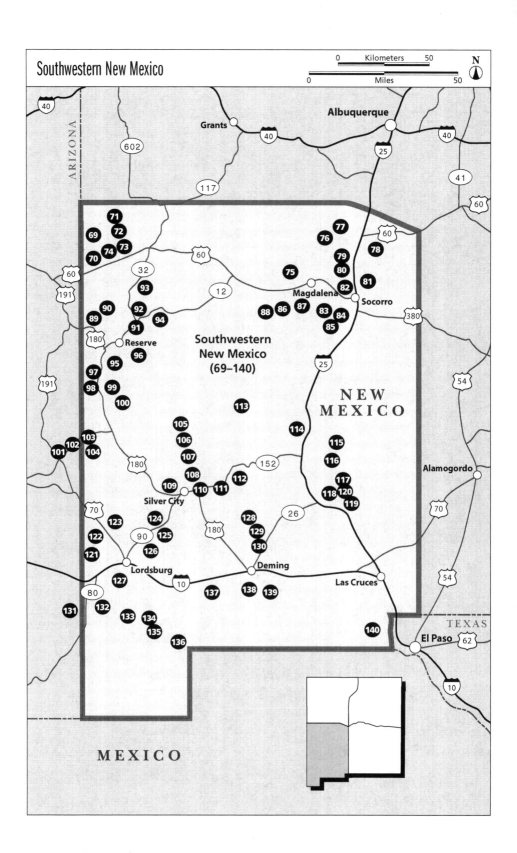

Red Hill

Land type: High desert.

GPS: N34° 19' 49" / W108° 57' 14".

Elevation: 6,965 feet.

Best time of year: March through November.

Land manager: Bureau of Land Management, Albuquerque District.

Material: Agate, petrified wood, jasper, crystals, and porcelain agate.

Tools: Geological hammer, spray bottle, and small shovel.

Vehicle: Any vehicle will do to the last turnoff, but if you want to drive the final 1.1 miles, four-wheel drive is recommended.

Precautions and restrictions: This is a very remote area. Be sure your vehicle is in good condition and that you are carrying enough water and fuel.

Special attractions: Stop and look around the lava flows on the way to the site. They are quite impressive. Red Cone volcanic mountain is an almost perfectly formed volcano that is also worth a stop and look. Zuni Salt Lake (see sites 71 and 72) is nearby.

Finding the site: This site is located northwest of Quemado near the Arizona border. From the west side of Quemado at the junction of Highway 32 and U.S. Highway 60, take US 60 west 23.2 miles and turn north on a well-graded gravel road just past milepost 11. Continue on this road for 2.9 miles, where you cross a cattle guard. After another 1.7 miles you will pass the cone of the volcanic red hill for which this area is named. Continue past the cone and after 1.3 miles you will pass an old log house and a road leading to a water tank on the left (west). On the right is a large lava flow, which continues for quite a few miles. Continue on this road for another 2.2 miles, at which point you will pass under the high arched gate for the Red Cone Ranch. Drive another 0.6 mile to the ranch. Bear to the right as you are passing through the ranch and go another 0.7 mile, where you will see a corral and water tank on the right and a rough road on the left (west). Turn left (west), drive about 0.6 mile, and cross a wash. This is the start of the collecting area, which continues for quite a distance.

Rockhounding

We never found the porcelain agate that is reportedly in this area, but what we did locate was sure worth the trip. All types of chalcedony—everything from

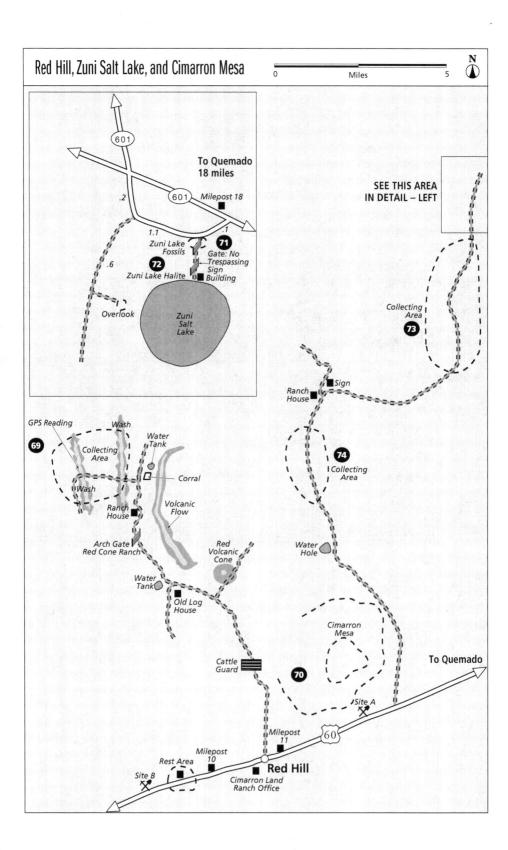

Red Hill, Zuni Salt Lake, and Cimarron Mesa

N

0   Miles   5

**SEE THIS AREA
IN DETAIL – LEFT**

601

To Quemado
18 miles

601   *Milepost 18*

.2

1.1   .1

*Zuni Lake
Fossils*   **71**

.6   **72**   Gate: No
Trespassing
Sign

Zuni Lake Halite   Building

Overlook   *Zuni
Salt
Lake*

*Collecting
Area*
73

Sign

*Ranch
House*

GPS Reading   *Wash*

69   *Collecting
Area*   *Water
Tank*

Corral

Wash

*Ranch
House*

*Volcanic
Flow*

74
*Collecting
Area*

*Arch Gate
Red Cone Ranch*

*Red
Volcanic
Cone*

*Water
Hole*

*Water
Tank*

*Old Log
House*

*Cimarron
Mesa*

To Quemado

*Cattle
Guard*

70

Site A

*Milepost
11*

60

Rest Area
*Milepost
10*

Site B   **Red Hill**

*Cimarron Land
Ranch Office*

Many kinds of chalcedony can be found at Red Hill.

clear and white to moss of all colors to banded and true black agate—can be picked up here, in addition to jasper, crystals, and petrified wood.

While we found nothing in the two washes we crossed, the slopes into the second one, located about 1.3 miles down the final road, contained abundant agate. One curious piece had a hole right through the middle. The GPS coordinates are for this wash.

U.S. Highway 60 Wood

See map on page 116.
Land type: High desert.
GPS: N34° 12' 54" / W108° 53' 24" (site B).
Elevation: 7,291 feet.
Best time of year: March through November.
Land manager: New Mexico Department of Transportation.
Material: Jasper, petrified wood, and agate.
Tools: Geological hammer, small shovel, and spray bottle.
Vehicle: Any.
Precautions and restrictions: Park well off the road. There is lots of private land in the area, so either get permission or stick to the right-of-way.
Special attractions: Stop and look around the lava flows on the gravel road leading to site 69. They are quite impressive. Also along this road is Red Cone volcanic mountain, an almost perfectly formed volcano. Zuni Salt Lake (see sites 71 and 72) is nearby.
Finding the site: This area is located near the Arizona border on U.S. Highway 60. From Quemado, drive 20.5 miles on US 60 to a large road cut. This is site A. To get to site B, continue 2.8 miles to Red Hill, which is marked by a small building on the left (south) with a sign reading CIMARRON LAND RANCH OFFICE. Drive another mile to a rest area on the right (north) side of the road just past milepost 10. This is site B.

Rockhounding

Many of the road cuts in this area have agates, petrified wood, and jasper. At site A we found some colorful and cuttable wood in a very short time. In about fifteen minutes of looking around site B, we found three pieces of nice cuttable petrified wood, one agate, and a pretty chunk of jasper. If you have time, try other road cuts.

Zuni Salt Lake Fossils

See map on page 116.
Land type: High desert.
GPS: N34° 27' 30" / W108° 46' 07".
Elevation: 6,392 feet.
Best time of year: March through November.
Land manager: New Mexico Department of Transportation.
Material: Marine fossils, including brachiopods and crinoid stems.
Tools: Geological hammer, sledgehammer, chisels, screwdriver, and goggles.
Vehicle: Any.
Precautions and restrictions: Always wear goggles when hammering or chiseling. Get permission before entering private land.
Special attractions: Stop and look around the lava flows on the gravel road leading to site 69. They are quite impressive. Also along this road is Red Cone volcanic mountain, an almost perfectly formed volcano.
Finding the site: This area is located northwest of Quemado. From Quemado at the junction of U.S. Highway 60 and Highway 601, drive northeast on Highway 601 for 18 miles. Just before reaching milepost 18, turn left (south) onto an unmarked gravel road. Drive 0.1 mile and turn left again onto another gravel road, which leads down to Zuni Lake. You will reach a locked gate, where you can park.

Rockhounding

We found well-formed marine fossils at the side of the road before the first locked gate. Pieces were abundant and relatively easy to remove.

Zuni Salt Lake Halite

See map on page 116.
Land type: High desert.
GPS: N34° 27' 15" / W108° 46' 47" (overlook).
Elevation: 6,409 feet.
Best time of year: March through November.
Land manager: The Zuni Nation.
Material: Halite.
Tools: Geological hammer and small shovel.
Vehicle: Any.
Precautions and restrictions: This is private land and closed to collecting without permission from the Zuni Nation.
Special attractions: Stop and look around the lava flows on the gravel road leading to site 69. They are quite impressive. Also along this road is Red Cone volcanic mountain, an almost perfectly formed volcano.

Zuni Salt Lake halite crystals.

Finding the site: This area is located northwest of Quemado. From Quemado at the junction of U.S. Highway 60 and Highway 601, drive northeast on US 601 for 18 miles. Just before reaching milepost 18, turn left (south) onto an unmarked gravel road. Drive 0.1 mile and turn left again onto another gravel road, which leads down to Zuni Salt Lake. You will reach a locked gate, where you can park.

A great view of Zuni Salt Lake can be had by driving back out on the gravel road and turning left (south). Go 1.1 miles and turn left (south) again. Continue 0.6 mile to a parking area on the left, which overlooks the lake.

Rockhounding

Fine halite crystals may be found here, but they can only be collected with permission from the Zuni Nation. Care must be taken to keep them intact for the ride home.

Zuni Salt Lake Quartzite and Jasper

See map on page 116.

Land type: High desert.

GPS: N34° 25' 24" / W108° 46' 59".

Elevation: 6,442 feet.

Best time of year: March through November.

Land manager: New Mexico Department of Transportation.

Material: Quartzite and jasper.

Tools: Geological hammer, small shovel, spray bottle, and goggles.

Vehicle: Any vehicle is OK except when road is wet or in disrepair.

Precautions and restrictions: Wear goggles and be very careful when chipping. Park off the road and be aware of private land.

Special attractions: Stop and look around the lava flows on the gravel road leading to site 69. They are quite impressive. Also along this road is Red Cone volcanic mountain, an almost perfectly formed volcano. Zuni Salt Lake (see sites 71 and 72) is nearby.

Finding the site: This site is northwest of Quemado near the Arizona border. From Quemado, drive 20.1 miles on U.S. Highway 60 and turn right (north) onto an unmarked, well-graded gravel road. As you drive north, you will notice a large mesa on the left (west)—this is Cimarron Mesa. Continue north to milepost 16.8. The collecting area begins at about milepost 14 and extends to milepost 18.

Rockhounding

This location provides the rockhound with some beautiful multicolored quartzite that polishes well. It makes extremely handsome cabs as well as other decorative pieces such as bookends.

Many of the pieces have to be chipped to see the striking interior colors. Try to hammer off small pieces and then spray the fracture. Some of the chunks of this tumbled quartzite are quite large, over five pounds. Take a close look at the reds—some are jasper.

Cimarron Mesa

See map on page 116.

Land type: High desert.

GPS: N34° 19' 01" / W108° 51' 02".

Elevation: 6,532 feet.

Best time of year: March through November.

Land manager: New Mexico Department of Transportation.

Material: Petrified limb casts and agates.

Tools: Geological hammer, small shovel, and spray bottle.

Vehicle: Any.

Precautions and restrictions: Park where you will not block the road.

Special attractions: Stop and look around the lava flows on the gravel road leading to site 69. They are quite impressive. Also along this road is Red Cone volcanic mountain, an almost perfectly formed volcano. Zuni Salt Lake (see sites 71 and 72) is nearby.

Finding the site: This site is northwest of Quemado near the Arizona border. From Quemado, drive 20.1 miles on U.S. Highway 60 and turn right (north) onto an unmarked, well-graded gravel road. As you drive north, you will notice a large mesa on the left (west)—this is Cimarron Mesa. Continue north 7.8 miles to the collecting area.

Rockhounding

Nice limb casts can be found in this area. They make very interesting display pieces but may not be solid enough to cut. We also found a few agates.

Most of the land in this area is private, but plenty of wood can be found in the right-of-way. Each time the road is graded, more shows up. Just because we only give one site doesn't mean that it is the only place the wood could be found. Stop often and look around.

Silver Hill

Land type: Rolling grassland.

GPS: N34° 08' 22" / W107° 17' 08".

Elevation: 5,529 feet.

Best time of year: All year, though there may be snow in winter.

Land manager: Cibola National Forest.

Material: Chrysocolla, azurite, barite, agate, druzy quartz, quartz crystals, apatite, descloizite, anglesite, and chalcocite.

Tools: Geological hammer, spray bottle, and small shovel.

Vehicle: Any vehicle will do if you park at the gate.

Precautions and restrictions: The final road can be very rough. Watch for snakes during warm weather.

Special attractions: The Mineral Museum of the New Mexico Bureau of Mines and Mineral Resources in Socorro and the Box Car Museum in Magdalena are well worth a visit. See a large array of radio telescopes just west of Magdalena at the National Radio Astronomy Observatory.

A pile of tailings at Silver Hill.

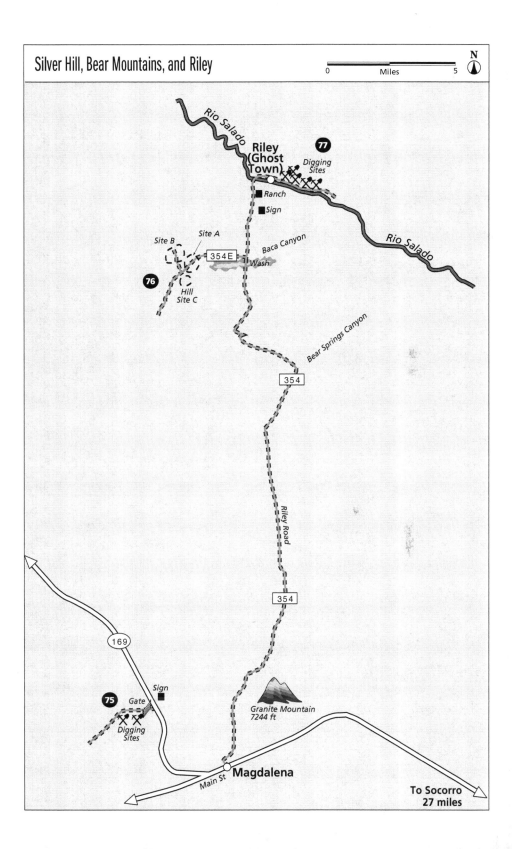

Silver Hill, Bear Mountains, and Riley

0   Miles   5

N

Rio Salado

Riley (Ghost Town)

77

Digging Sites

■ *Ranch*

■ *Sign*

Rio Salado

Site B   *Site A*

354E   Baca Canyon

Wash

76

Hill Site C

Bear Springs Canyon

354

Riley Road

354

169

Sign ■

75 *Gate* ■

× ×

Digging Sites

Granite Mountain
7244 ft

Magdalena

Main St

**To Socorro
27 miles**

Finding the site: This mining area is located just northwest of the town of Magdalena. From Magdalena, take U.S. Highway 60 west to Highway 169. Go 3.3 miles northwest on Highway 169 to a gate on the left (west) and rough tracks leading into the hills, just before a Forest Service sign on the right. Pass through the gate (be sure to close it behind you) and either park on the side or continue on for about 0.1 mile. You will see several pits off to the left.

Rockhounding

The Silver Hill mining district consists mainly of some small open pits. The prospect holes here produced copper and silver. To find the holes, one must hike around and explore the area. During a half-hour inspection of the two pits, we found minerals such as copper ores, apatite, barite, druzy quartz, some agate, and one specimen of well-formed barite crystals. There were also large, colorful garden rocks with coatings of copper ore. If you are willing to do some searching and digging, these prospects could yield worthwhile specimens relating to copper and silver ore. Also reported at this location are descloizite, anglesite, and chalcocite. With all these minerals around, a spray bottle of water is essential to help identify them.

Bear Mountains

See map on page 125.

Land type: Rocky, hilly mixed grassland and desert.

GPS: Site A: N33° 59' 11" / W106° 59' 29". Site B: N34° 20' 24" / W107° 15' 11". Site C: N34° 20' 21" / W107° 15' 10".

Elevation: 5,900 feet (site A).

Best time of year: March through October.

Land manager: Cibola National Forest.

Material: Quartz, petrified wood, hematite, and agate.

Tools: Spray bottle, geological hammer, and small shovel optional.

Vehicle: Any vehicle will do to the second forest road, but if you want to drive the final mile, four-wheel drive is recommended.

Special attractions: The Mineral Museum of the New Mexico Bureau of Mines and Mineral Resources in Socorro and the Box Car Museum in Magdalena are well worth a visit. See a large array of radio telescopes just west of Magdalena at the National Radio Astronomy Observatory.

Finding the site: From Main Street in Magdalena, turn right (north) onto Forest Road 354 (Riley Road), which leads to the ghost town of Riley. Continue 17.4 miles; at this point, take the second left (the first left leads into an arroyo) onto Forest Road 354E (Baca Canyon Road). This is a four-wheel-drive track, but you can park about 0.8 mile up it and hike the approximate mile to the collecting area.

Rockhounding

After turning onto FR 354E, we were able to continue for 0.8 mile in four-wheel drive, at which point the road became extremely rough. There's a good parking area about that distance up FR 354E, and we found small pieces of petrified wood next to our vehicle when we got out.

Site A is located about another mile up the road from the parking area. Hike both sides of the road, heading toward the hills in the distance, to find petrified wood, colorful quartzite, agate, and small pieces of carnelian. Turn at the tracks off to the right and walk uphill to explore site B, where nice pieces of hematite can be found. Site C is a small hill to the left of the main road. Lots of wood and hematite are found all around the base of the hill.

The above is only a sampling of what's available here. Continue on this road to many other collecting locations.

Riley

See map on page 125.

Land type: High desert.

GPS: N32° 22' 51" / W107° 13' 43".

Elevation: 5,529 feet.

Best time of year: All year.

Land manager: Bureau of Land Management, Albuquerque District; private.

Material: Barite, jasper, agate, and agate nodules.

Tools: Geological hammer and small shovel.

Vehicle: Any vehicle will do if you wade across the river, but four-wheel drive is necessary if you want to drive across.

Precautions and restrictions: Don't cross the river by vehicle or on foot if the water is high and flowing fast.

Special attractions: The Mineral Museum of the New Mexico Bureau of Mines and Mineral Resources in Socorro and the Box Car Museum in Mag-

The ghost town of Riley.

dalena are well worth a visit. See a large array of radio telescopes just west of Magdalena at the National Radio Astronomy Observatory.

Finding the site: This area is located in the Cibola National Forest. From Main Street in Magdalena, turn right (east) onto Forest Road 354 (Riley Road), which leads to the ghost town of Riley. After about 19 miles, the road forks at a sign for Santa Rita Ranches. Keep left and go 0.8 mile to a right turn just past a ranch. Drive to the river and cross if you have high-clearance four-wheel drive and the water is not high. Make the first right after river and drive a few hundred yards to the town site.

Rockhounding

Jasper, agate, and agate nodules have been reported at this site, but we only found a few pieces of barite. It seems like most of the dumps have been covered or spread out. However, this is a great site to visit to get a historical perspective of the area.

Contreras

Land type: High desert.
GPS: N34° 23' 30" / W106° 48' 21".
Elevation: 4,713 feet.
Best time of year: October through April.
Land manager: New Mexico Department of Transportation.
Material: Petrified wood, agate, jasper, unakite, and quartzite.
Tools: Geological hammer, small shovel, and spray bottle.
Vehicle: Any.
Precautions and restrictions: Park well off the road and be mindful of private property.
Special attractions: See a large array of radio telescopes just west of Magdalena at the National Radio Astronomy Observatory, and learn about the historic Camino Real at El Camino Real International Heritage Center, located south of Socorro. In Socorro, the New Mexico Institute of Mining and Technology Museum's collection of over 15,000 specimens is a must-see. View the Abó, Gran Quivira, and Quarai ruins at the Salinas Pueblo Missions National Monument in Mountainair. The Bosque del Apache National Wildlife Refuge near Socorro offers bird- and wildlife-viewing opportunities. It is possible to see bald eagles, sandhill cranes, snow geese, and many other bird species here.
Finding the site: This site is located east of Interstate 25, south of Albuquerque and north of Socorro. Take I-25 to exit 175 east and U.S. Highway 60. Drive east on US 60 for 2.1 miles and cross the Rio Grande. Continue 1 more mile and turn right (south) onto Highway 304. This is the start of the collecting area, which continues about 6 miles.

Rockhounding

We only looked along the roadside in this area and found a number of rather small pieces of petrified wood, agate, jasper, and colorful quartzite. A few were large enough to cut. We cannot say that the stones were overabundant here.

One oddity that we found was unakite, which is the unofficial gemstone of the state of Virginia. It is a mixture of pink or orange feldspar and green epidote, and it cuts into some very pretty gemstones that are used for pendants and earrings. Keep in mind that we only found two pieces about 2 inches by 3 or 4 inches.

Much of the land here is private, so keep to the right-of-way. A number of washes cross the road, and there is plenty of gravel for you to look through.

San Lorenzo Arroyo

Land type: High desert.
GPS: N34° 13' 51 / W106° 57' 51".
Elevation: 4,967 feet.
Best time of year: October through May.
Land manager: Bureau of Land Management, Albuquerque District.
Material: Agate, barite, rhyolite, calcite, petrified wood, jasper, granite, and chrysoprase.
Tools: Geological hammer, small shovel, and spray bottle.
Vehicle: Any vehicle will probably do unless you want to take the road to the wash, in which case four-wheel drive is necessary.
Precautions and restrictions: This is a remote area. Be sure your vehicle is in good shape and that you are carrying enough water and fuel to get yourself out of trouble.
Special attractions: See a large array of radio telescopes just west of Magdalena at the National Radio Astronomy Observatory, and learn about the historic Camino Real at El Camino Real International Heritage Center, located south of Socorro. In Socorro, the New Mexico Institute of Mining and Technology Museum's collection of over 15,000 specimens is a must-see. View the Abó, Gran Quivira, and Quarai ruins at the Salinas Pueblo Missions National Monument in Mountainair. The Bosque del Apache National Wildlife Refuge near Socorro offers bird- and wildlife-viewing opportunities. It is possible to see bald eagles, sandhill cranes, snow geese, and many other bird species here.
Finding the site: This site is located off Interstate 25 about 50 miles south of Albuquerque and 6 miles north of Socorro. From I-25, take exit 156 west at Lemitar. Turn right (north) onto the frontage road and drive 4.6 miles. Turn left (west) here on the dirt road that you will see before the frontage road makes a sharp turn right (east) and goes under the interstate. Follow this dirt road for 0.3 mile, at which point the road divides. If you are in a two-wheel-drive vehicle, keep to the left (south). The right (north) fork leads to a sandy wash that should not be attempted unless you have four-wheel drive. The south (left) fork is rocky, hilly, and rough, but a two-wheel-drive vehicle in good shape should be able to negotiate this road. In either case, continue on for 1 mile, at which point the two roads come together again. Go another 0.7 mile to a junction, then bear right (north) toward the arroyo. In 0.1 mile you will see a sign that says you are entering San Lorenzo Canyon. This is the start of the collecting area. Do not drive any farther unless you have four-wheel drive.

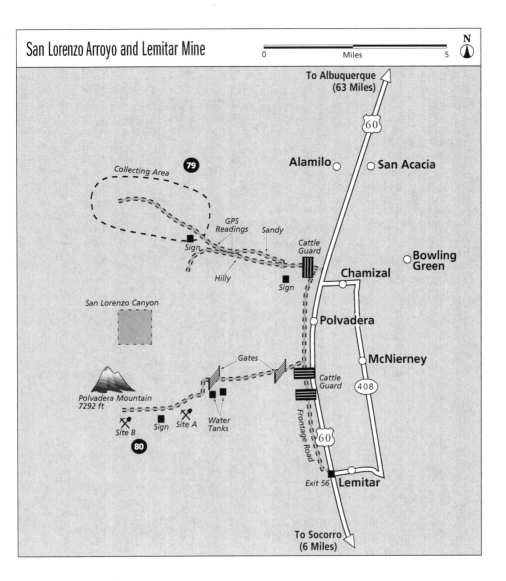

Rockhounding

The GPS coordinates were taken 0.5 mile into the arroyo, but the collecting area extends for at least 3 more miles. Material is not all that abundant here, but good quantities of nice agate and other minerals can be collected if the rockhound spends a bit of time looking. One of the nicest things we found was a single piece of a translucent red barite. Some of the agates were banded and others were clear or white, with some displaying swirled areas of black and/or red. We also found rhyolite, calcite, petrified wood, jasper, granite, and chrysoprase at this site.

Lemitar Mine

See map on page 132.

Land type: Mountainous desert.

GPS: Site A: N34° 11' 36" / W106° 57' 55". Site B: N34° 11' 24" / W106° 58' 39".

Elevation: Site A: 5,382 feet. Site B: 5,866 feet.

Best time of year: March through May, October, and November.

Land manager: Bureau of Land Management, Albuquerque District.

Material: Barite, fluorite, chalcopyrite, wulfenite, galena, quartz crystals, pegmatite, siderite, sphalerite, iron pyrite, malachite, hemimorphite, cerrussite, and anglesite.

Tools: Geological hammer, goggles, sledgehammer, chisels, and small shovel.

Vehicle: We do not advise it, but a two-wheel-drive vehicle may be able to make it to the second gate. After that, four-wheel drive is definitely required.

Precautions and restrictions: This is a remote area. Be sure your vehicle is in good shape and that you are carrying enough water and fuel to get yourself out of trouble.

Special attractions: See a large array of radio telescopes just west of Magdalena at the National Radio Astronomy Observatory, and learn about the historic Camino Real at El Camino Real International Heritage Center, located south of Socorro. In Socorro, the New Mexico Institute of Mining and Technology Museum's collection of over 15,000 specimens is a must-see. View the Abó, Gran Quivira, and Quarai ruins at the Salinas Pueblo Missions National Monument in Mountainair. The Bosque del Apache National Wildlife Refuge near Socorro offers bird- and wildlife-viewing opportunities. It is possible to see bald eagles, sandhill cranes, snow geese, and many other bird species here.

Finding the site: The mine is located off Interstate 25 about 50 miles south of Albuquerque and 6 miles north of Socorro. From I-25, take exit 156 west at Lemitar. Turn north (right) onto the frontage road and drive 2.7 miles (you will cross a cattle guard just before this distance). Turn left (west) onto a rough, sandy road and drive 2.1 miles to the second gate. There is a water tank just before the gate on the left (south) side of the road. Immediately after the gate you will come to a junction. Turn left (south) here and continue 0.1 mile past another water tank on your left (east). Take the faint tracks leading off to the west (right) and continue up the hillside another 0.2 mile to site A on your left (south). Site B is another 0.7 mile farther.

Rockhounding

Fluorite cubes can be found at site A, but better ones are available at site B. We found some up to ½ inch on a side. Most cubes at both sites are very clear but colorless. At site B you will find beautiful chunks of pink, salmon, and white barite lying all over the ground. Some of it is swirled with colors, and you should be able to find material solid enough to cut and polish.

Explore carefully to find other minerals. In addition to the barite and fluorite, we found chalcopyrite, wulfenite, galena, quartz crystals, pegmatite, and siderite, while others have reported sphalerite, iron pyrite, malachite, hemimorphite, cerrussite, and anglesite.

Socorro

Land type: Rolling hills, high desert.
GPS: N34° 06' 57" / W106° 47' 57".
Elevation: 5,049 feet.
Best time of year: All year.
Land manager: Bureau of Land Management, Albuquerque District.
Material: Crinoid stems, brachiopods, bivalves (some with shell intact), marine snails, and many other marine fossils that have not yet been identified.
Tools: Geological hammers, picks, and goggles.
Vehicle: Any vehicle is fine in dry weather; otherwise, four-wheel drive is needed since the road could get muddy and a few washes cross it.
Special attractions: See a large array of radio telescopes just west of Magdalena at the National Radio Astronomy Observatory, and learn about the historic Camino Real at El Camino Real International Heritage Center, located south of Socorro. In Socorro, the New Mexico Institute of Mining and Technology Museum's collection of over 15,000 specimens is a must-see. View the Abó, Gran Quivira, and Quarai ruins at the Salinas Pueblo Missions National Monument in Mountainair. The Bosque del Apache National Wildlife Refuge near Socorro offers bird- and wildlife-viewing opportunities. It is possible to see bald eagles, sandhill cranes, snow geese, and many other bird species here.
Finding the site: This site is located in the hills northeast of Socorro. From Socorro, take Interstate 25 north about 2 miles to the Escondida exit (exit 152) and continue north on Highway 408 for 1.5 miles. Turn right (east) and follow the Quebradas National Backcountry Byway signs 0.9 mile to Pueblito, crossing some railroad tracks and the Rio Grande River. Turn right (south) and proceed 1 mile, then turn left (east) and drive 4.9 miles, at which point you will come to a large wash crossing the road. Park on the side and hike north down the wash toward the hills on the right.

Rockhounding

Millions of years ago this area was covered by a sea. Today the only evidence of its former existence are the numerous marine fossils found in the hills. Walk along the wash and make forays up the sides of the hills, carefully inspecting any areas that have a lot of small broken pieces. Larger sections can be shattered to reveal hidden fossils, but we found it more productive to just closely inspect areas of broken-up rock and pebbles. Your eyes will become accustomed to the shape and size of the specimens.

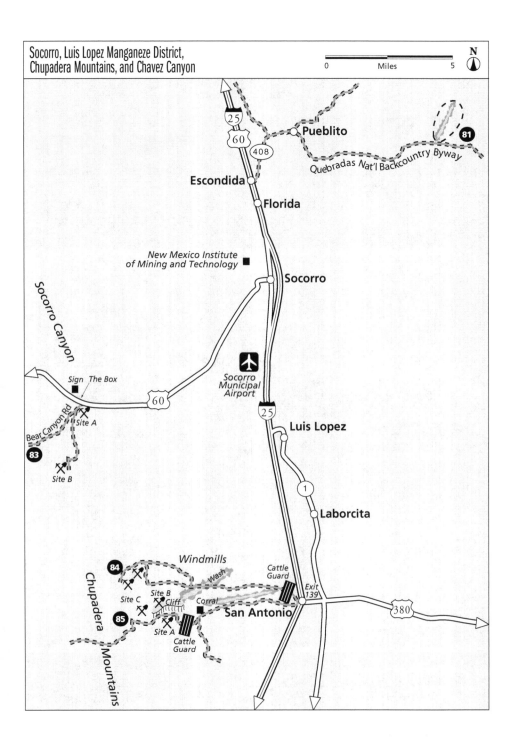

N

0   Miles   5

Pueblito

81

Quebradas Nat'l Backcountry Byway

Escondida

Florida

New Mexico Institute
of Mining and Technology

Socorro

Socorro Canyon

Sign   The Box

Bear Canyon Rd

Site A

Socorro
Municipal
Airport

83

Site B

Luis Lopez

1

Laborcita

Windmills

Wash

Cattle
Guard

Exit
139

84

Site B

Cliff

Corral

Site C

San Antonio

380

Chupadera Mountains

85

Site A

Cattle
Guard

Socorro Peak Mining District

Land type: Mountainous desert.

Best time of year: March through October.

Land manager: Energetic Materials Research Testing Center.

Material: Quartz, fluorite, barite, calcite, galena, cerussite, wulfenite, and vanadinite.

Tools: Geological hammer, spray bottle, and shovel.

Vehicle: Four-wheel drive.

Precautions and restrictions: No collecting allowed without permission. Beware of mine shafts in the area and loose rocks on the tailings piles.

Special attractions: See a large array of radio telescopes just west of Magdalena at the National Radio Astronomy Observatory, and learn about the historic Camino Real at El Camino Real International Heritage Center, located south of Socorro. In Socorro, the New Mexico Institute of Mining and Technology Museum's collection of over 15,000 specimens is a must-see. View the Abó, Gran Quivira, and Quarai ruins at the Salinas Pueblo Missions National Monument in Mountainair. The Bosque del Apache National Wildlife Refuge near Socorro offers bird- and wildlife-viewing opportunities. It is possible to see bald eagles, sandhill cranes, snow geese, and many other bird species here.

Finding the site: This site is north of Socorro. Get directions when applying for permission to collect (see below).

Rockhounding

The silver ore mined here was primarily chlorargyrite, but this area also produced lead, zinc, and copper. Socorro Peak can be seen from the city—it is the mountain with the big *M* on it. The mines are now controlled by Energetic Materials Research Testing Center (EMRTC). They have an office on the New Mexico Tech campus, and you must get permission in person from them to collect. Permits are usually only granted for weekends and holidays.

We did not go to this site because our timing was off. It sure sounds interesting, though—with reports of quartz, fluorite, barite, calcite, galena, cerussite, wulfenite, and vanadinite—and we'll definitely try the next time we're in the area.

Luis Lopez Manganese District

See map on page 136.

Land type: Rugged hills and high desert.

GPS: Site A: N34° 06' 58" / W106° 47' 41". Site B: N34° 00' 19" / W106° 59' 35" (start of four-wheel-drive road to site).

Elevation: Site A: 5,050 feet. Site B: 5,492 feet.

Best time of year: October through April.

Land manager: Bureau of Land Management, Albuquerque District; Cibola National Forest.

Material: Agate, carnelian, calcite, azurite, malachite, chalcopyrite, psilomelane, pyrolusite, hollandite, goethite, jasper, and rhodochrosite.

Tools: Geological hammers, picks, and goggles.

Vehicle: This is marginal two-wheel-drive territory with some walking. Four-wheel drive is preferred.

Precautions and restrictions: Use extreme caution due to mine shafts. This is not an area advised for children.

Special attractions: See a large array of radio telescopes just west of Magdalena at the National Radio Astronomy Observatory, and learn about the historic Camino Real at El Camino Real International Heritage Center, located south of Socorro. In Socorro, the New Mexico Institute of Mining and Technology Museum's collection of over 15,000 specimens is a must-see. View the Abó, Gran Quivira, and Quarai ruins at the Salinas Pueblo Missions National Monument in Mountainair. The Bosque del Apache National Wildlife Refuge near Socorro offers bird- and wildlife-viewing opportunities. It is possible to see bald eagles, sandhill cranes, snow geese, and many other bird species here.

Finding the site: This mining area is located about 8 miles west of Socorro. From Socorro, take U.S. Highway 60 west and begin clocking mileage at the western edge of town from the sign giving the mileage to Magdalena (26 miles). Turn left (south) at 6.8 miles onto Bear Canyon Road (sign at entrance reads the box). Site A begins at a large parking area on the left 0.1 mile from US 60. To get to site B, follow the road 0.4 mile from site A to an unmarked rough road and turn left (east). Proceed 1.2 miles to an uphill fork on the right. This road can be negotiated with a rugged high-clearance vehicle, or just walk the 0.3 mile to the old mine site.

Rockhounding

At site A we found small but nice pieces of agate and jasper in the parking area as well as the hillsides. Some of this is carnelian. Site B is the operation at the end of the road where many diggings are found. You can sort through the rubble or chip, with caution, at the walls. We found nice botryoidal psilomelane and some that even appears to be pseudomorphs after pyrite. The black psilomelane also forms as a fine druzy on some surfaces. Keep your eyes open for the clear cubic crystals of calcite that are also in the area. Also reported found at this site are various copper ores, hollandite, goethite, rhodochrosite, and pyrolusite.

Chupadera Mountains

See map on page 136.

Land type: Mountainous high desert.

Best time of year: October through April.

Land manager: Bureau of Land Management, Albuquerque District.

Material: Psilomelane, hematite, agate, and quartz crystals.

Tools: Gads, geological hammer, picks, chisels, goggles, and small shovel.

Vehicle: Two-wheel drive is marginal to the washout in the road; four-wheel-drive needed beyond that.

Precautions and restrictions: Probable bad road.

Special attractions: See a large array of radio telescopes just west of Magdalena at the National Radio Astronomy Observatory, and learn about the historic Camino Real at El Camino Real International Heritage Center, located south of Socorro. In Socorro, the New Mexico Institute of Mining and Technology Museum's collection of over 15,000 specimens is a must-see. View the Abó, Gran Quivira, and Quarai ruins at the Salinas Pueblo Missions National Monument in Mountainair. The Bosque del Apache National Wildlife Refuge near Socorro offers bird- and wildlife-viewing opportunities. It is possible to see bald eagles, sandhill cranes, snow geese, and many other bird species here.

Finding the site: This area is located about 10 miles southwest of Socorro. From Socorro, take Interstate 25 south about 10 miles to the San Antonio exit (exit 139). Immediately after exiting and before going under the interstate, look for a gravel road on the right. Turn right onto the gravel road, go over the cattle guard, and continue for 0.1 mile. (If you are coming from the south, the exit will take you right into San Antonio. You must turn around and drive under the interstate. Immediately after passing under the bridge, make a left onto the gravel road, drive over the cattle guard, and proceed for 0.1 mile. If you miss the turn, you will end up on the interstate heading south.) Turn right toward the mountains and continue 5.3 miles. The diggings can be seen on the left side of the road, but the best collecting is another 0.8 mile up the road on the northern side of the ridge.

Rockhounding

We never made it to this site, as the gravel road was washed out at an arroyo and we did not have time to hike. We got as far as 2.7 miles up the mine road. However, we were able see the diggings in the distance and found psilomelane, hematite, agate, and quartz crystals in the road surrounding washes.

Chavez Canyon

See map on page 136.

Land type: Mountainous high desert.

GPS: Site A: N33° 54' 51" / W106° 56' 33". Site B: N33° 54' 49" / W106° 56' 45". Site C: N33° 54' 46" / W106° 57' 09".

Elevation: Site A: 5,032 feet. Site B: 5,023 feet. Site C: 5,061 feet.

Best time of year: October through April.

Land manager: Bureau of Land Management, Albuquerque District, Cibola National Forest.

Material: Agate, jasper, chalcedony roses with and without crystals, quartz crystal clusters, rhyolite, calcite, alabaster, opalite, suspected garnet, and rhyolite nodules filled with crystals.

Tools: Gads, geological hammer, picks, chisels, small shovel, and goggles.

Vehicle: Two-wheel drive is marginal until the wash in Chavez Canyon, then four-wheel drive is required.

Precautions and restrictions: See a large array of radio telescopes just west of Magdalena at the National Radio Astronomy Observatory, and learn about the historic Camino Real at El Camino Real International Heritage Center, located south of Socorro. In Socorro, the New Mexico Institute of Mining and Technology Museum's collection of over 15,000 specimens is a must-see. View the Abó, Gran Quivira, and Quarai ruins at the Salinas Pueblo Missions National Monument in Mountainair. The Bosque del Apache National Wildlife Refuge near Socorro offers bird- and wildlife-viewing opportunities. It is possible to see bald eagles, sandhill cranes, snow geese, and many other bird species here.

Finding the site: From Socorro, take Interstate 25 south about 10 miles to the San Antonio exit (exit 139). Immediately after exiting and before going under the interstate, look for a gravel road on the right. Turn right onto the gravel road, go over the cattle guard, and continue for 0.1 mile. (If you are coming from the south, the exit will take you right into San Antonio. You must turn around and drive under the interstate. Immediately after passing under the bridge, make a left onto the gravel road, drive over the cattle guard, and proceed for 0.1 mile. If you miss the turn, you will end up on the interstate heading south.) Keep to the left (south) and go another 0.3 mile, at which point the road makes a sharp right (west); follow this road for 2.5 more miles to a corral. In another 0.1 mile, make a right (north) turn onto a smaller, more

Agate can be found at this site in Chavez Canyon.

rugged road. Proceed on this road for another 1.3 miles into Chavez Canyon. At this point you can either park your car and hike or continue on with a four-wheel-drive vehicle to the rockhounding sites. This is also a nice spot to set up camp if you plan to spend the night.

Rockhounding

To get to site A from the parking/camping area, proceed another 0.1 mile to where the road meets a large wash. Directly to the right is a high ridge with seams of white alabaster and calcite visible on its upper reaches. Some of the material may erode out of the cliff, and therefore a careful search of the cliff's foot might be productive. This is excellent carving material.

To reach site B from site A, continue another 0.2 mile to the entrance of a small canyon on the right. Hike about a quarter mile up the canyon and then hike several hundred feet into a smaller canyon to the right. Here we found an opalite deposit yielding a range of colors from pink/beige to dark brown. Some of the material is fractured, but with careful searching, one can find enough opalite that will take a nice polish.

The GPS coordinates for site C were taken at the base of the hill, which contains some of the finest and largest chalcedony roses we have ever found. Some of them measure 8 inches across. This area is 0.5 mile past site B. Climb up the side of the mountain, and soon you will encounter many roses—just keep climbing until you find some. They appear to be most numerous near the summit. Some of these roses are coated with crystals, and some need to be chiseled out of the matrix. Leave a part of the country rock attached. In this form, they make very attractive display pieces. The larger roses are suitable for cutting.

Moss agate can also be found here and on the opposite side of the mountain. In addition, we picked up jasper, quartz crystal clusters, rhyolite, and bright red gemstones that we think are garnets. Others have reported rhyolite nodules filled with crystals.

Magdalena Nitt and North Graphic Mines

Land type: Mountainous forest.

Best time of year: April though October.

Land manager: Bill's Gem and Mineral Shop.

Material: Iron ores, smithsonite, azurite, barite, pyrite, and bornite.

Tools: Geological hammer, small shovel, and spray bottle.

Vehicle: Any.

Special attractions: The Box Car Museum in Magdalena is well worth a visit. See a large array of radio telescopes just west of Magdalena at the National Radio Astronomy Observatory, and learn about the historic Camino Real at El Camino Real International Heritage Center, located south of Socorro. In Socorro, the New Mexico Institute of Mining and Technology Museum's collection of over 15,000 specimens is a must-see. The Bosque del Apache National Wildlife Refuge near Socorro offers bird- and wildlife-viewing opportunities. It is possible to see bald eagles, sandhill cranes, snow geese, and many other bird species here.

Precautions and restrictions: This is a pay site. No collecting allowed without a permit.

Finding the site: These mines are located south of Magdalena. Get directions when you pick up your pass (see below).

Rockhounding

These two mines are famous for producing fine specimens of smithsonite and other minerals. The dumps contain plenty of pyrite and small amounts of the other minerals listed above. Most folks who have paid the fee and spent some time at these mines feel they got their money's worth.

To buy permits, contact Bill's Gem and Mineral Shop at (505) 854-2236. The shop is located next to the Ponderosa restaurant off U.S. Highway 60 in Magdalena.

Kelly Mine

Land type: Mountainous forest.

Best time of year: April through October.

Land manager: Tony's Rock Shop.

Material: Iron ores, smithsonite, azurite, barite, pyrite, and bornite.

Tools: Geological hammer and shovel.

Vehicle: Any.

Special attractions: The Box Car Museum in Magdalena is well worth a visit. See a large array of radio telescopes just west of Magdalena at the National Radio Astronomy Observatory, and learn about the historic Camino Real at El Camino Real International Heritage Center, located south of Socorro. In Socorro, the New Mexico Institute of Mining and Technology Museum's collection of over 15,000 specimens is a must-see. The Bosque del Apache National Wildlife Refuge near Socorro offers bird- and wildlife-viewing opportunities. It is possible to see bald eagles, sandhill cranes, snow geese, and many other bird species here.

Precautions and restrictions: This is a pay site. No collecting allowed without a permit.

Finding the site: The mine is located south of Magdalena. Pick up directions when you get your permit.

Rockhounding

This mine is famous for producing fine specimens of smithsonite and the other minerals listed. The dumps contain plenty of pyrite and small amounts of the other listed minerals. Most folks who have paid the fee and spent some time here feel they got their money's worth.

To buy permits, contact Tony's Rock Shop at (760) 742-1356 or (505) 854-2401. The shop is located on Kelly Road in Magdalena.

Highway 52 Agate

Land type: High desert.
GPS: N33° 45' 06" / W107° 40' 22".
Elevation: 6,907 feet.
Best time of year: All year.
Land manager: Bureau of Land Management, Albuquerque District.
Material: Agate, chalcedony roses, and botryoidal psilomelane.
Tools: Geological hammer and spray bottle.
Vehicle: Any.
Special attractions: The Mineral Museum of the New Mexico Bureau of Mines and Mineral Resources in Socorro and the Box Car Museum in Magdalena are both well worth a visit.
Finding the site: This site is in the hilly area southwest of Magdalena. From Magdalena, drive 19 miles west on U.S. Highway 60, then 27.2 miles south on Highway 52. Cross the wash and park.

Rockhounding

Walk both sides of the wash that crosses the road, examining the rocks carefully. We found chalcedony roses, some with nice druzy overlay; black agate; and clear and white agate with swirls of red. All of these pieces were large enough for cutting and would make beautiful cabochons.

San Francisco River Agate

Land type: Mountainous forest.

GPS: N33° 49' 35" / W109° 01' 19".

Elevation: 7,431 feet.

Best time of year: May through October.

Land manager: Gila National Forest.

Material: Agate, jasper, geodes, and amethyst crystals.

Tools: Geological hammer and small shovel.

Vehicle: Any.

Precautions and restrictions: It can get very icy and cold here in the winter. The climb down to the river could be muddy and difficult, and the rocks are very slippery. As you hike along the river, be aware of your limitations and turn around before you get too tired.

Special attractions: The artsy town of Reserve is known for its shops and galleries. We were told that there are petroglyphs in the area; ask around for directions. The old mining town of Mogollon is nearby (see site 100), and the Catwalk National Recreation Trail is located near Glenwood.

Finding the site: From Silver City, drive northwest on U.S. Highway 180 into the town of Luna. From the post office on the right (north), continue west on US 180 another 4.3 miles. At this point you would have crossed a bridge over the San Francisco River and come to a Forest Service road (no number apparent) on the right (north). Turn here and park, or drive down a bit if the road is acceptable.

Rockhounding

We only found a few pieces of agate and geode material (jasper) at this site. It is not the place to go if you are looking for a big supply of material, but it's reported that hiking in both directions along the river might yield some nice pieces, including amethyst geodes.

North of Luna

Land type: Mountainous forest.
GPS: N33° 50' 39" / W108° 58' 09" (site A).
Elevation: 7,548 feet.
Best time of year: May through October.
Land manager: Gila National Forest.
Material: Agate, quartz crystals, jasper, amethyst crystals, and geodes.
Tools: Geological hammer, small shovel, and spray bottle.
Vehicle: Any vehicle will do unless the roads are icy and snow-covered.
Precautions and restrictions: It can get very icy and cold here in winter, and the roads can be completely snow-covered. This is bear and cougar country, so take the proper precautions.
Special attractions: The artsy town of Reserve is known for its shops and galleries. We were told that there are petroglyphs in the area; ask around for directions. The old mining town of Mogollon is nearby (see site 100), and the Catwalk National Recreation Trail is located near Glenwood.
Finding the site: This area is located in the hills north of Luna, not far from the Arizona border. From Silver City, drive northwest on U.S. Highway 180 to the town of Luna. Immediately after reaching the southern outskirts of town, turn right (north) onto County Road B007. Proceed 2.2 miles to Forest Road 220 and turn left (west). Site A is at 0.6 mile and site B is at 1.1 miles.

Rockhounding

The given sites are places we selected at random. Site A is the area where we located substantial amounts of agate, but you could probably stop almost anywhere along this road and find some material. The majority of the agate that we found was either clear or white and banded; however, many have nice inclusions that make fine cut pieces. We also found quartz crystals and jasper at this site, and others have reported amethyst crystals and geodes.

Largo Canyon

Land type: Hilly high desert.
GPS: N33° 46' 15" / W108° 42' 38".
Elevation: 6,124 feet.
Best time of year: March through November.
Material: Agate and jasper.
Tools: Small shovel and geological hammer.
Vehicle: Any vehicle is OK to the wash, but four-wheel drive is probably needed after that.
Precautions and restrictions: Take a good look at the wash before trying to cross it with a two-wheel-drive vehicle.
Special attractions: The artsy town of Reserve is known for its shops and galleries. We were told that there are petroglyphs in the area; ask around for directions. The old mining town of Mogollon is nearby (see site 100), and the Catwalk National Recreation Trail is located near Glenwood.

Looking for agate in the wash at Largo Canyon.

Finding the site: This site is located north of Reserve. From Silver City, travel northwest on U.S. Highway 180 through the town of Alma, then continue another 25.8 miles to the junction of Highway 12. Turn right (northeast) onto Highway 12 and head toward Reserve, which is 7 miles ahead. Once in Reserve, at the junction of Highways 12 and 35, continue northeast on Highway 12. Travel 5.2 miles to County Road B013 on the left (west) and follow this road about 0.1 mile to where it crosses a large wash. Park before the wash.

Rockhounding

We found the best and the most numerous agates at the first crossing of the wash. Many were clear with nice dark inclusions. Make sure you look not only in the wash but also along the eroded areas on the slopes. We found a few more agates another couple tenths of a mile up the road but did not go any farther. This road becomes Forest Road 49 and crosses the wash a number of times. It may pay to do some exploring.

Lee Russell Canyon

Land type: Forested canyon.
GPS: N33° 54' 00" / W108° 38' 27".
Elevation: 6,077 feet.
Best time of year: May through October.
Land manager: Gila National Forest.
Material: Agate, agate nodules, partial geodes, jasper, and calcite.
Tools: Geological hammer and small shovel; spray bottle if the creek is dry.
Vehicle: Any.
Precautions and restrictions: There is private land in the area, and the rocks in the creek are slippery.
Special attractions: The artsy town of Reserve is known for its shops and galleries. We were told that there are petroglyphs in the area; ask around for directions. The old mining town of Mogollon is nearby (see site 100), and the Catwalk National Recreation Trail is located near Glenwood.
Finding the site: This site is located north of Reserve. From Silver City, travel northwest on U.S. Highway 180 through the town of Alma, then continue another 25.8 miles to the junction of Highway 12. Turn right (northeast) onto Highway 12 and head toward Reserve, which is 7 miles ahead. Once in Reserve, at the junction of Highways 12 and 435, continue northeast on Highway 12 for 12 miles to Apache Creek. Turn left (north) at the Apache Creek Store onto Highway 32, drive 4.9 miles, and park on the left by a gate.

Rockhounding

The gate has been locked the several times we've been to this location, so be prepared to hike into the canyon. The walk is sure worth the effort, though. The road is public, but the first part of the trek is through private land. After passing into the national forest, you can start collecting. Excellent material can be found along the road and on the slopes leading down into the wash, as well as in the creek (wash) bed. We found first-class banded, fortification, and moss agate here. Some of the pieces are substantial in size and very solid, and they make excellent cabs and other decorative pieces. Some good-size pieces of geodes can also picked up, along with jasper and calcite.

Once we attempted to hike all the way to Turkey Flats, where we've heard a great variety of colorful material can be found. However, after a couple of miles, we ran out of trail and could not figure out the route.

Highway 32 Material

Land type: Mountainous forest.
GPS: N34° 03' 38" / W108° 39' 05" (site A).
Elevation: 8,056 feet.
Best time of year: April through October.
Land manager: New Mexico Department of Transportation.
Material: Agate, jasper, crystals, and geode segments.
Tools: Geological hammer, small shovel, and spray bottle.
Vehicle: Any.
Precautions and restrictions: Highway 32 can be icy and snow-covered in winter. Be sure to pull well off the highway when looking for material, and be careful of loose rock around the slides.
Special attractions: The artsy town of Reserve is known for its shops and galleries. We were told that there are petroglyphs in the area; ask around for directions. The old mining town of Mogollon is nearby (see site 100), and the Catwalk National Recreation Trail is located near Glenwood.
Finding the site: This collecting area runs from Apache Creek to Quemado, north of Reserve. From Silver City, travel northwest on U.S. Highway 180 through the town of Alma, then continue another 25.8 miles to the junction of Highway 12. Turn right (northeast) onto Highway 12 and head toward Reserve, which is 7 miles ahead. Once in Reserve, at the junction of Highways 12 and 435, continue northeast on Highway 12 for 12 miles to Apache Creek. Turn left (north) at the Apache Creek Store onto Highway 32. Site A is 18.2 miles from Apache Creek and site B is at 24.5 miles.

Rockhounding

Site A is located at a New Mexico Department of Highways rest area. Agates can be found in the woods as well as the road cuts. Most are white or clear, but some have interesting inclusions. Site B is a road cut 24.5 miles north of Apache Creek. We found some incredible pieces of agate nodules in this area. Some were quite large, measuring over 6 inches, and many had carnelian as agate and crystal inclusions.

We actually stopped at a number of other cuts, some very close to Apache Creek. Just about all of them had some agate, including many pieces that were banded and had moss inclusions. It seems the agate peters out soon after site B. Both A and B yielded jasper, crystals, and geode segments.

Sand Canyon

Land type: High desert.

Best time of year: March through November.

Land manager: Gila National Forest.

Material: Agate and jasper.

Tools: Small shovel, geological hammer, and spray bottle.

Vehicle: The road is rough but can be driven with a rugged two-wheel-drive vehicle.

Precautions and restrictions: There is some private land in the area. The road is very rocky and rough in places.

Special attractions: The artsy town of Reserve is known for its shops and galleries. We were told that there are petroglyphs in the area; ask around for directions. The old mining town of Mogollon is nearby (see site 100), and the Catwalk National Recreation Trail is located near Glenwood.

Finding the site: This site is located north of Reserve. From Silver City, travel northwest on U.S. Highway 180 through the town of Alma, then continue another 25.8 miles to the junction of Highway 12. Turn right (northeast) onto Highway 12 and head toward Reserve, which is 7 miles ahead. Once in Reserve, at the junction of Highways 12 and 435, continue northeast on Highway 12 for 12 miles to Apache Creek and then another 0.8 mile to County Road B017. Make a right (southeast) onto CR B017 and cross a cattle guard, after which you turn left (east). Continue 1.1 miles to a wash crossing and begin looking for agate.

Rockhounding

We included this site because we heard that good agate can be found here. We did find a few small white pieces at the wash crossing, along with some jasper. At some point after crossing the wash, you enter national forest land and the road becomes Forest Road 289. At 1.8 miles the road forks; take Forest Road 249 on the right. Perhaps if one was to drive farther, more agates could be found.

Leggett Peak

Land type: Mountainous forest.
GPS: N38° 42' 41" / W108° 54' 30".
Elevation: 7,188 feet.
Best time of year: April through October.
Land manager: Gila National Forest.
Material: Agate, jasper, calcite, quartz crystals, and amethyst crystals.
Tools: Large shovel, bucket of water, geological hammer, and large pick.
Vehicle: Any.
Precautions and restrictions: It could be snow-covered, cold, and very icy here in winter.
Special attractions: The artsy town of Reserve is known for its shops and galleries. We were told that there are petroglyphs in the area; ask around for directions. The old mining town of Mogollon is nearby (see site 100), and the Catwalk National Recreation Trail is located near Glenwood.
Finding the site: This mountainous area is located south of Luna. From Silver City, take U.S. Highway 180 northwest to Alma, then continue another 29.6 miles on US 180. You will see a pull-off on the right and an undrivable dirt road heading up the hill. Park here.

Rockhounding

You'll find a great deal of agate lying around as float right in the parking area on both sides of the barbed-wire fence. As you follow the fence down, you will notice a few tracks on the other side heading off toward the mountain. Climb over or crawl under the fence and proceed up the washed-out road. Almost immediately you will see a large mound of dirt blocking the road. If you dig into this, you'll find substantial agates in a wide variety of patterns and colors. Many more can be located by digging in the loose soil on the uphill side of the road. We found dendritic, porcelain, white, clear, moss, and golden agate, as well as pieces of geodes with crystals. Some had light amethyst crystals.

The downward slope on the other side of US 180 contains more agate. We found a beautiful amethyst crystal here.

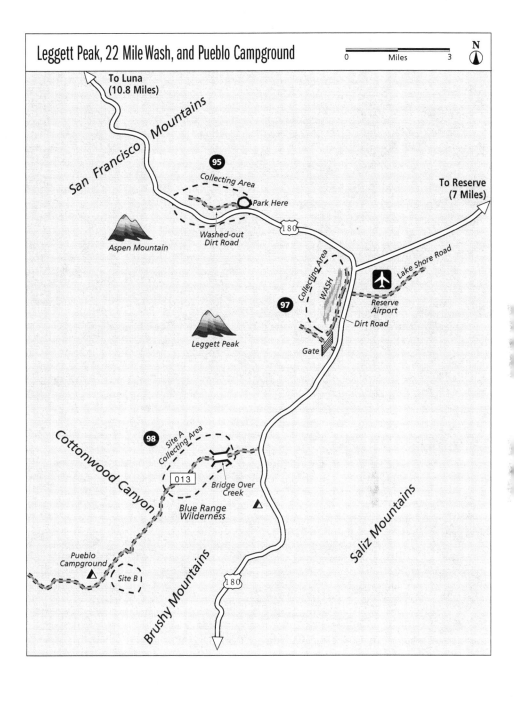

Leggett Peak, 22 Mile Wash, and Pueblo Campground

N

0   Miles   3

To Luna
(10.8 Miles)

San Francisco Mountains

95

Collecting Area

Park Here

Washed-out
Dirt Road

Aspen Mountain

180

To Reserve
(7 Miles)

Lake Shore Road

Collecting Area

WASH

97

Reserve
Airport

Dirt Road

Gate

Leggett Peak

98

Site A
Collecting Area

013

Bridge Over
Creek

Cottonwood Canyon

Blue Range
Wilderness

Saliz Mountains

Pueblo
Campground

Site B

Brushy Mountains

180

Frisco

Land type: Sloping high desert.
GPS: N33° 40' 41" / W108° 46' 31".
Elevation: 5,646 feet.
Best time of year: March through November.
Land manager: Gila National Forest.
Mineral: Agate, jasper, granite, and bubbly chalcedony.
Tools: Geological hammer and small shovel.
Vehicle: Any vehicle will do if you wade across the creek.
Precautions and restrictions: The rocks in the creek are slippery, so be careful wading across. Do not cross the creek in your vehicle unless you are absolutely sure it can make it.
Special attractions: The artsy town of Reserve is known for its shops and galleries. We were told that there are petroglyphs in the area; ask around for directions. The old mining town of Mogollon is nearby (see site 100), and the Catwalk National Recreation Trail is located near Glenwood.
Finding the site: This site is located just south of Reserve. From Silver City, travel northwest on U.S. Highway 180 through the town of Alma, then continue another 25.8 miles to the junction of Highway 12. Turn right (northeast) onto Highway 12 and head toward Reserve, which is 7 miles ahead. In Reserve, turn right (south) onto Highway 435 and travel 2.8 miles through Frisco to a left (east) turn toward Negrito Creek. Continue 0.3 mile to the creek and either park here or drive across the creek and park. Use judgment before crossing the creek, since the water might be high and flowing rapidly.

Rockhounding

We did not find a whole lot at this location, but did pick up enough to pique our interest. Perhaps when the water is low and a lot of exploring can be done along both sides of the creek, more material can be located. Jasper and white and yellow agates with inclusions were among the material we found. Perhaps the most interesting rocks we picked up were the tumbled pieces of fine-looking granite containing large blue and red patches resembling colorful pegmatite material. They make fine decorative pieces when cut and polished. Others have reported bubbly chalcedony in the area.

Looking for Negrito Creek agate near Frisco.

Parking can be a problem at this site. The only place to park unobtrusively is about 100 yards on the right before reaching the creek. On the left, parking can be found right at the creek, but four- wheel drive would be necessary to ensure getting out.

22 Mile Wash

See map on page 155.
Land type: Hilly forest.
GPS: N33° 40' 20" / W108° 52' 04".
Elevation: 6,265 feet.
Best time of year: April through November.
Land manager: Gila National Forest.
Material: Agate, quartz crystals, calcite, and jasper.
Tools: Small shovel and geological hammer.
Vehicle: Any vehicle will do up to the dirt road, at which point four-wheel drive is recommended.
Precautions and restrictions: Beware of snakes in summer. The roads can be icy in winter.
Special attractions: The artsy town of Reserve is known for its shops and galleries. We were told that there are petroglyphs in the area; ask around for directions. The old mining town of Mogollon is nearby (see site 100), and the Catwalk National Recreation Trail is located near Glenwood.
Finding the site: This area is northwest of Silver City and south of Luna. From Silver City, drive northwest on U.S. Highway 180 to Alma, then continue on US 180 for 24.9 miles, at which point you will notice a wash and an unpaved road on the left (west). Either park at the gate or open it and drive in.

Rockhounding

Park anywhere along the dirt road and explore the wash and the road for a variety of agates, jasper, and crystal-filled geode pieces. We found red and gold jasper with white banding, agate nodules with white and blue banding, porcelain agate, and a banded amber agate similar to the variety we found around Cook Inlet in Alaska. Chalcedony roses, some coated with druzy crystals, as well as some moss and plume agate were among the treasures we picked up.

The wash continues for a quite a distance. We walked about a mile and did not run out of material. Do not neglect the slopes on either side of the wash.

Pueblo Campground

See map on page 155.

Land type: Mountainous forest.

GPS: N33° 37' 56" / W108° 54' 47" (site A).

Elevation: 6,195 feet (site A).

Best time of year: April through October.

Land manager: Gila National Forest.

Material: Labradorite, agate, hypersthene, and bytownite.

Tools: Geological hammer, sledgehammer, and goggles.

Vehicle: Four-wheel drive is needed if you go all the way to the campground.

Precautions and restrictions: Always wear goggles when hammering—you want to be able to see all the beautiful stones you find. We noticed bear droppings in the area, and this is also cougar country. Keep your campsite clean, and take the proper precautions.

Special attractions: The artsy town of Reserve is known for its shops and galleries. We were told that there are petroglyphs in the area; ask around for directions. The old mining town of Mogollon is nearby (see site 100), and the Catwalk National Recreation Trail is located near Glenwood.

Finding the site: This area is northwest of Silver City and south of Luna. From Silver City, take U.S. Highway 180 northwest to Alma, then continue on US 180 an additional 21.8 miles. Turn left (west) on County Road 013 toward Pueblo Campground. Site A is at 1.1 miles. Site B is the Pueblo Campground at 6.1 miles.

Rockhounding

We found labradorite and agate at this location, while others have reported hypersthene and bytownite. The gemstones are found in the gas cavities of rhyolite. Some claim they are most abundant in the reddish rocks with white specks, but we seemed to find just as many in gray stones. The gems are reported to be as large as 1 inch; however, the largest we found were closer to ⅛ inch.

Most guidebooks say you should drive to site B, the Pueblo Campground. However, we found the gems a short way after turning onto CR 013. Pick up any rock that appears to have cavities and smash it with a hammer. Many will display internal crystals that have the chatoyance of labradorite. The rhyolite polishes quite well, and in combination with a few labradorite crystals, the cabs make very handsome jewelry pieces.

Mogollon Road

Land type: Rolling hills, high desert.
GPS: N33° 22' 33" / W108° 53' 00".
Elevation: 5,165 feet.
Best time of year: March through November.
Land manager: New Mexico Department of Transportation.
Material: Chalcedony roses, agate, and rhyolite.
Tools: Geological hammer and small shovel.
Vehicle: Any.
Precautions and restrictions: Park well off the road.
Special attractions: The artsy town of Reserve is known for its shops and galleries. We were told that there are petroglyphs in the area; ask around for directions. The old mining town of Mogollon is nearby (see site 100), and the Catwalk National Recreation Trail is located near Glenwood.
Finding the site: This site is northwest of Silver City. From the junction of Highway 78 and U.S. Highway 180, head north on US 180 for 18.8 miles. Turn right (east) onto Highway 159 (Mogollon Road) and drive 1.4 miles to the site.

Rockhounding

We found this site upon failing to get to Mogollon. We took a walk along the road and started finding agates that ranged from chalcedony roses to moss agate. A very nice banded rhyolite that takes a nice polish was also picked up. The location was randomly picked, and we're sure there are many others like it in this area.

Mogollon Road

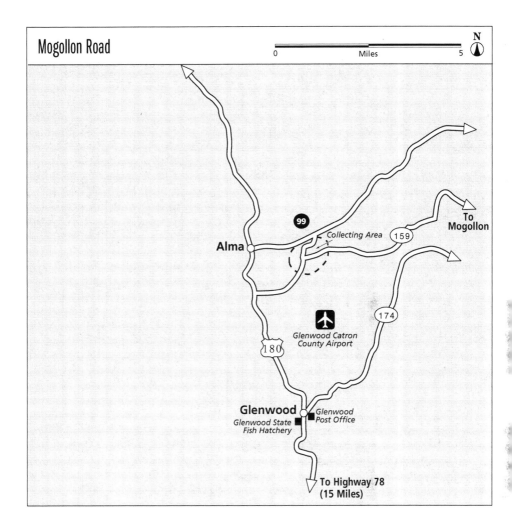

0   Miles   5

N

99

Alma

Collecting Area

159

To
Mogollon

174

Glenwood Catron
County Airport

180

Glenwood

Glenwood
Post Office

Glenwood State
Fish Hatchery

To Highway 78
(15 Miles)

Mogollon

Land type: Mountainous forest.

Best time of year: May through October.

Land manager: New Mexico Department of Transportation.

Material: Fluorite, calcite, pyrite, chalcopyrite, chalcocite, malachite, azurite, native gold and silver, bornite, galena, and argentite.

Tools: Geological hammer and spray bottle.

Vehicle: Four-wheel drive.

Precautions and restrictions: There are open mining pits in the area, so be careful.

Special attractions: The artsy town of Reserve is known for its shops and galleries. We were told that there are petroglyphs in the area; ask around for directions. The Catwalk National Recreation Trail is located near Glenwood.

Finding the site: This site is northwest of Silver City, deep in the Gila National Forest. From the junction of Highway 78 and U.S. Highway 180, head north on US 180 for 18.8 miles. Turn right (east) onto Highway 159 and drive about 10 miles.

Rockhounding

We never made it to this site because, as is often the case, the road was closed. The material listed above was reported by others. A lot of dumps and mines are supposed to be obvious here. Many of them are posted, but some come down to the road, and those can be searched.

Highway 78 Agate

Land type: Rolling desert hills.

GPS: N32° 59' 15" / W109° 10' 49" (site A).

Elevation: 4,051 feet (site A).

Best time of year: All year.

Land manager: New Mexico Department of Transportation.

Material: White agate, black agate, and agate nodules.

Tools: Geological hammer and small shovel.

Vehicle: Any.

Precautions and restrictions: There might be some claims in the area, so look for stakes. Park well off the road.

Special attractions: A good view of Morenci Copper Mine can be had at a pull-off along Highway 78. This is a very scenic area.

Finding the site: This site is northwest of Lordsburg. From the junction of Arizona Highways 191 and 78, travel east 4.2 miles on Highway 78 to site A. Site B is at 7.6 miles.

Rockhounding

This location is actually in Arizona but is very close to the border. You may not find a lot of material here, but some nice pieces can be picked up with a bit of walking. Explore the low hills on both sides of the road. We found about a dozen small pieces, including chalcedony roses (some with crystals), in about a half hour of searching. We also found some black agate at site B. The two sites we give were selected randomly. Stop often along Highway 78 and look around.

State Line Zeolites

Land type: Mountainous desert.
GPS: N33° 02' 55" / W109° 06' 06".
Elevation: 5,635 feet.
Best time of year: All year.
Land manager: New Mexico Department of Transportation.
Material: Zeolites.
Tools: Geological hammer, sledgehammer, chisels, gads, hard hat, and goggles.
Vehicle: Any.
Precautions and restrictions: Park your vehicle well off the road. Be very careful of falling rocks and slides around the road cut. Always wear a hard hat when working near the cliffs and goggles when chiseling or hammering.
Special attractions: A good view of Morenci Copper Mine can be had at a pull-off along Highway 78. This is a very scenic area.
Finding the site: This site is located northwest of Lordsburg. From the junction of Arizona Highways 191 and 78, travel 11.8 miles on Highway 78 to the road cut.

Zeolites can be found near the Arizona–New Mexico state line northwest of Lordsburg.

Rockhounding

This site is in Arizona but is very close to the border. We found nice micro-mounts of various zeolites in basalt and rhyolite vesicles, many of which were loose in the talus of the road cut. The best specimens can be obtained by chiseling carefully. Be sure to bring bubble wrap or tissue paper to protect your treasures. More zeolites can be found in similar road cuts all the way to the state line.

State Line Chalcedony

Land type: Mountainous forest.
GPS: N33° 05' 10" / W109° 04' 45".
Elevation: 6,029 feet.
Best time of year: March through November.
Land manager: Bureau of Land Management, Las Cruces District.
Material: Chalcedony roses.
Tools: Geological hammer and small shovel.
Vehicle: Any.
Precautions and restrictions: Be very careful of other vehicles on Highway 78, as it is very curvy and you might not be seen. Park only at the pull-offs.
Special attractions: A good view of Morenci Copper Mine can be had at a pull-off along Highway 78. This is a very scenic area.
Finding the site: This site is northwest of Lordsburg. From the junction of Arizona Highways 191 and 78, go 16.5 miles east on Highway 78 to the road cut.

Rockhounding

This site is actually in Arizona but is very close to the border. The material is in a large road cut that extends over a half mile. Some of the chalcedony roses can be quite large and covered with crystals. Many are dirty and difficult to spot, so walk very slowly and be observant. On the north side, the chalcedony roses are eroding out of the basalt that was cut away when the road was built. On the south side, search the slope below the road.

Mule Creek

Land type: Mountainous forest.
GPS: Site A: N33° 06' 12" / W109° 03' 21". Site B: N33° 06' 22" / W109° 02' 41".
Elevation: Site A: 5,750 feet. Site B: 5,984 feet.
Best time of year: March through November.
Land manager: Gila National Forest.
Material: Apache tears.
Tools: Geological hammer and small shovel.
Vehicle: Any.
Precautions and restrictions: Park well off the road. Black bears and cougars occupy the area, so take the proper precautions and keep your campsite clean.
Special attractions: A good view of Morenci Copper Mine can be had at a pull-off along Highway 78. This is a very scenic area.
Finding the site: This site is located northwest of Lordsburg. From the junction of Arizona Highways 191 and 78, travel east on Highway 78 for 19.1 miles to site A. Site B is at mile 20, which is the state line. Site C is located at milepost 20.6.

Rockhounding

This area is difficult to search because of the pine needle litter. In addition, the Apache tears are very weathered, making them even more difficult to spot. One has to be very observant and look for a glint of black or a flash of light. We only found three small tears at site A. Sites B and C were more productive because the tears were out in the open. The tears here are rather opaque but take a nice polish when tumbled and make handsome display pieces or even jewelry.

We chose these sites at random. It is possible to finds Apache tears anywhere in the area—simply walk slowly through the woods.

Little Bear Canyon

Land type: Mountainous forest.
GPS: Site A: N33° 15' 05" / W108° 15' 02". Site B: N33° 16' 19" / W108° 15' 36".
Elevation: Site A: 6,242. Site B: 5,680 feet.
Best time of year: May through October.
Land manager: Gila National Forest.
Material: Banded, clear, gray, and white agate; chunks of calcite; rhyolite "flower rock"; and possibly labradorite.
Tools: Geological hammer, spray bottle, goggles, gads, and chisels (optional).
Vehicle: Any vehicle is OK, except during inclement weather. Large RVs and trailers are not recommended.
Precautions and restrictions: The road from Silver City is very windy and could be icy or snow-covered; only limited maintenance is performed on weekends and nights during winter. Do not attempt the trip with a two-wheel-drive vehicle during inclement weather, especially in winter. The road is not recommended for large RVs or trailers. Know your hiking limits—it may not seem too bad going down to the river, but remember that you will have to hike back up, hopefully with some rocks. Little Bear Canyon is subject to flash floods, so be aware of the weather report since parts of the canyon are very steep and it would be difficult to escape if the water rises suddenly. It is illegal to collect within the boundaries of the Gila Cliff Dwelling National Monument; however, not far down the trail is the beginning of the Gila National Forest, where it is legal to collect small amounts for personal use.
Special attractions: Gila Hot Springs Pools and Campground can be found along the West Fork of the Gila River. Gila Cliff Dwellings National Monument has a fine display of local minerals. Silver City has lots of downtown galleries and is also home to the Royal Scepter Museum and Rock Shop. Tyrone Copper Mine has a display and observation area on Tyrone Thomas Road (Forest Road 136). Travel about 11.7 miles south on Highway 90 from its junction with Broadway in Silver City. Turn right (west) onto Tyrone Thomas Road (FR 136). The observation deck can be seen when you turn.
Finding the site: From Silver City at the junction of U.S. Highway 180 and Highway 15, head north on Highway 15 toward the Gila Cliff Dwellings National Monument. The road is paved but narrow and winding, with very sharp curves and steep hillsides. At mile 42 you will be in the national monument.

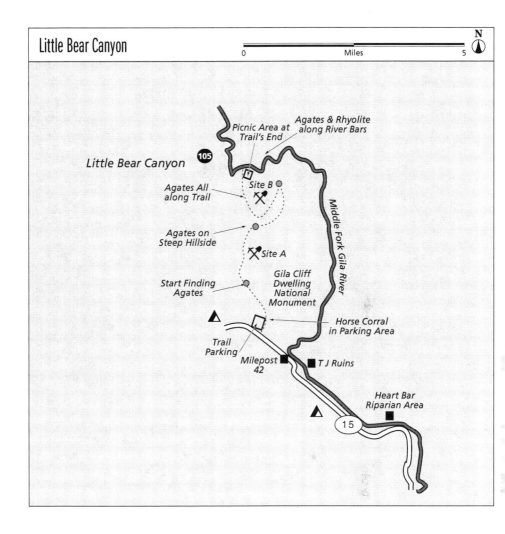

Little Bear Canyon

Agates & Rhyolite along River Bars

Picnic Area at Trail's End

Little Bear Canyon

Agates All along Trail

Site B

Agates on Steep Hillside

Site A

Middle Fork Gila River

Gila Cliff Dwelling National Monument

Start Finding Agates

Horse Corral in Parking Area

Trail Parking

Milepost 42

T J Ruins

Heart Bar Riparian Area

Turn left (west) and go 0.5 mile, then turn right (north) at a sign for TJ Corral Trail and park. The trailhead to Little Bear Canyon will be on your left.

Rockhounding

Located in the Gila National Forest, this is a great hike for those who are able to do an 8-mile-plus trek over moderately steep terrain. The Little Bear Canyon trailhead is in the Gila National Monument (no rock collecting here, please), but the trail soon enters the national forest. A great variety of agate and rhyolite can be found on the trail, which is about 4 miles long. It gains about 1,000 feet in elevation from the parking area to the top and then drops another 1,500 feet to the bottom of the canyon at the Gila River.

After passing the national monument/national forest boundary, you will start noticing pieces of white agate here and there. The trail at site A runs along the side of a steep hill. Look through the rocks carefully—many are agates, some quite large. Most are white or white/clear, but some have very interesting inclusions. These cut into fine gemstones.

Soon after site A, the path descends steeply into the canyon. You can follow the trail or the wash. Either way, many agates will be encountered. Some are white or clear or a combination thereof. Many are banded, and some have moss patterns. We have not found too many that can be described as very colorful, but the layers and inclusions more than make up for the lack of pigment.

After passing through the canyon, you will arrive at the banks of the Middle Fork Gila River (site B). Look for gravel bars, where more agates can be found. Also keep your eyes open for what we termed "flower rock," which is a rhyolite with patches that look like flower petals—something like daisies. They can be difficult to spot, but after cutting and polishing, the floral patterns will become apparent.

You will easily be able to spot the granite if it is sunny. Many pieces have small crystals that display a labradorescence. We do not know if the material is labradorite, but it seems to be. This also cuts into fine cabs.

When you are ready to call it a day, put the best material you collected in a backpack and start heading back up the trail. But don't take too much—the hike back is quite steep.

Gila River

Land type: Forested mountains.

GPS: N33° 11' 05" / W108° 12' 30".

Elevation: 5,574 feet.

Best time of year: April though November.

Land manager: Gila National Forest.

Material: Thomsonite, naturalite, stilbite, mesolite, chabazite, calcite, zeolites, and quartz crystals.

Tools: Geological hammer, sledgehammer, chisels, gads, and goggles.

Vehicle: Any vehicle is OK, except during inclement weather. Large RVs and trailers are not recommended.

Precautions and restrictions: Be very careful around cliffs and road cuts, as loose material from above can fall and cause severe injury or worse. It is best to take a piece of fallen rock and move away from the precipice before attempting to split it. Always wear goggles. The road from Silver City is very windy and could be icy or snow-covered; only limited maintenance is performed on weekends and nights during winter. Do not attempt the trip with a two-wheel-drive vehicle during inclement weather, especially in winter. The road is not recommended for large RVs or trailers.

Special attractions: Gila Hot Springs Pools and Campground can be found along the West Fork of the Gila River. Gila Cliff Dwellings National Monument has a fine display of local minerals. Silver City has lots of downtown galleries and is also home to the Royal Scepter Museum and Rock Shop. Tyrone Copper Mine has a display and observation area on Tyrone Thomas Road (Forest Road 136). Travel about 11.7 miles south on Highway 90 from its junction with Broadway in Silver City. Turn right (west) onto Tyrone Thomas Road (FR 136). The observation deck can be seen when you turn.

Finding the site: This area is along the Gila River a few miles south of the Gila Cliff Dwellings National Monument. From Silver City at the junction of U.S. Highway 180 and Highway 15, travel north on Highway 15 for 38.3 miles. The zeolites are in the basalt in a deep narrow canyon on the left (west) side of the road.

Rockhounding

At this site we found thomsonite, naturalite, stilbite, and mesolite, while others have reported chabazite, calcite, and quartz crystals. The zeolites are found

Zeolites can be found in the basalt along the Gila River.

throughout the basalt in this area, but they can be difficult to remove without destruction. Most are great-looking micromounts, but a few up to an inch can be discovered with a lot of work and diligence. The mesolite appears as white balls and threads. Chabazite is in the form of white to colorless rhombs, and the stilbite appears as radiating sheaves. Small spheres of thomsonite are common.

Much of what is on the surface is eroded, but chunks having any evidence of the minerals on the face will probably have a lot more internally. Split suspect specimens very gently by chiseling a small hole and softly tapping a gad into the opening until the rock breaks. Then carefully break off excess matrix from the specimen.

Copperas Peak

Land type: Mountainous forest.
GPS: Site A: N33° 06' 01" / W108° 11' 34". Site B: N33° 07' 00" / W108° 11' 58".
Elevation: Site A: 6,721 feet. Site B: 7,349 feet.
Best time of year: April through October.
Land manager: Gila National Forest.
Material: Moss agate, banded agate, and chalcedony roses with opal coating.
Tools: Geological hammer.
Vehicle: Any vehicle is OK, except during inclement weather. Large RVs and trailers are not recommended.
Precautions and restrictions: The road from Silver City is very windy and could be icy or snow-covered; only limited maintenance is performed on weekends and nights during winter. Do not attempt the trip with a two-wheel-drive vehicle during inclement weather, especially in winter. The road is not recommended for large RVs or trailers.
Special attractions: Gila Hot Springs Pools and Campground can be found along the West Fork of the Gila River. Gila Cliff Dwellings National Monument has a fine display of local minerals. Silver City has lots of downtown galleries and is also home to the Royal Scepter Museum and Rock Shop. Tyrone Copper Mine has a display and observation area on Tyrone Thomas Road (Forest Road 136). Travel about 11.7 miles south on Highway 90 from its junction with Broadway in Silver City. Turn right (west) onto Tyrone Thomas Road (FR 136). The observation deck can be seen when you turn.
Finding the site: This site is north of Silver City. From Silver City at the junction of U.S. Highway 180 and Highway 15, follow Highway 15 north for 30.1 miles to site A and park at the pull-off on the right (east) side of the road. Site B is at 32 miles, and the pull-off is also on the right (east). Site C is the large rest area on the left (west) at Copperas Peak.

Rockhounding

We found a large number of agates at sites A and B, but we think they are all along this road, so don't limit yourself to only the mentioned spots. Most of the agates found were endowed with very interesting mossy patterns in black, red, green, and even blue, while others had fascinating and varied inclusions in many different colors. While these agates might not look attractive when picked up, after cutting and polishing, they make fine-looking gems for jewelry and other decorative pieces. One can also find some very colorful and opaque rhyolite in this area, which can be worked into nice pieces.

At site C we found beautiful chalcedony roses. Some of these are coated with small crystals and when cleaned make beautiful additions to a collection, while smaller ones can be used for jewelry. An attractive fine blue or white opalite coats some of the chalcedony roses. After parking at the rest area, hike down the slope and keep your eyes on the ground. The roses will soon be apparent.

Meerschaum Mining Area

Land type: Mountainous forest.

GPS: N33° 02' 23" / W108° 40' 48".

Elevation: 5,613 feet.

Best time of year: April through October.

Land manager: Gila National Forest.

Material: Meerschaum, agate, calcite clusters, and quartz crystals.

Tools: Geological hammer.

Vehicle: Any vehicle is OK, except during inclement weather. Large RVs and trailers not recommended.

Precautions and restrictions: The road from Silver City is very windy and could be icy or snow-covered; only limited maintenance is performed on weekends and nights during winter. Do not attempt the trip with a two-wheel-drive vehicle during inclement weather, especially in winter. The road is not recommended for large RVs and trailers.

Special attractions: Gila Hot Springs Pools and Campground can be found along the West Fork of the Gila River. Gila Cliff Dwellings National Monument has a fine display of local minerals. Silver City has lots of downtown galleries and is also home to the Royal Scepter Museum and Rock Shop. Tyrone Copper Mine has a display and observation area on Tyrone Thomas Road (Forest Road 136). Travel about 11.7 miles south on Highway 90 from its junction with Broadway in Silver City. Turn right (west) onto Tyrone Thomas Road (FR 136). The observation deck can be seen when you turn.

Finding the site: This mining area is located north of Silver City. In Silver City from the junction of U.S. Highway 180 and Highway 15, follow Highway 15 north for 25 miles. You will pass over a large wash, where the material can be found.

Rockhounding

Meerschaum is a soft, pure white mineral that is very lightweight. It was once in great demand for making fine pipes and decorative carved objects. There was even a time when meerschaum was more valuable than gold.

The mine was closed a long time ago, and today it is quite an arduous hike to get up to it. We found some nice pieces of meerschaum in the wash that crosses the road. Very nice agates, some coated with crystals, can also be picked up here.

Bear Mountain Fossils

Land type: Forested hills.
GPS: N32° 49' 26" / W108° 20' 18" (site A).
Elevation: 5,679 feet (site A).
Best time of year: March through November.
Land manager: Gila National Forest.
Material: Brachiopods, crinoid stems, and many other marine fossils; petrified wood, agate, chert, rhyolite, and jasper.
Tools: Geological hammer and small chisel or screwdriver.
Vehicle: Any vehicle is OK, except during inclement weather.
Precautions and restrictions: The forest road can be snow-covered and muddy at times.
Special attractions: Gila Hot Springs Pools and Campground can be found along the West Fork of the Gila River. Gila Cliff Dwellings National Monument has a fine display of local minerals. Silver City has lots of downtown galleries and is also home to the Royal Scepter Museum and Rock Shop. Tyrone

Fossil site at Bear Mountain, north of Silver City.

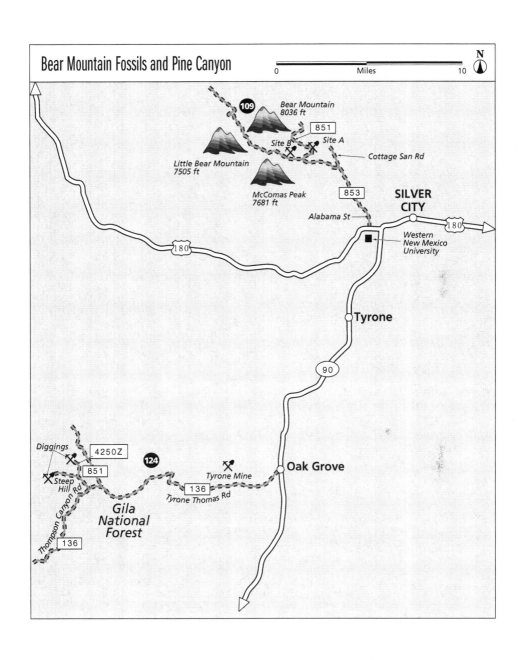

Bear Mountain Fossils and Pine Canyon

N

0   Miles   10

Bear Mountain
8036 ft

109

851

Site B   Site A

Cottage San Rd

Little Bear Mountain
7505 ft

McComas Peak
7681 ft

853

SILVER
CITY

Alabama St

180

Western
New Mexico
University

180

Tyrone

90

Diggings

4250Z

124

851

Tyrone Mine

Steep
Hill Rd

Oak Grove

136

Tyrone Thomas Rd

Gila
National
Forest

Thompson Canyon Rd

136

Copper Mine has a display and observation area on Tyrone Thomas Road (Forest Road 136). Travel about 11.7 miles south on Highway 90 from its junction with Broadway in Silver City. Turn right (west) onto Tyrone Thomas Road (FR 136). The observation deck can be seen when you turn.

Finding the site: This area is located a short distance northwest of Silver City. From the junction of Highway 90 and U.S. Highway 180, travel west on US 180 for 0.6 mile. Turn right (north) on Alabama Street (Forest Road 853). Travel 5.2 miles to Forest Road 851 and turn right (east). This is the location of site A. To get to site B, go another 0.4 mile on FR 853.

Rockhounding

At site A many fossils are present on the right hillside as soon as you turn onto FR 851. You can drive farther in on this road if you have a four-wheel-drive vehicle. Site B is located on the hillside to the right off FR 853 and requires some hiking and exploring of the surrounding area to find the material listed above.

Hanover-Fierro Mining Area

Land type: Hilly desert.

GPS: N32° 49' 53" / W108° 04' 43".

Elevation: 5,679 feet.

Best time of year: All year.

Land manager: New Mexico Department of Transportation.

Material: Chalcopyrite, magnetite, azurite, galena, hematite, chrysacolla, quartz, calcite, sphalerite, malachite, chalcosite, and cuprite.

Tools: Geological hammer and spray bottle.

Vehicle: Any.

Precautions and restrictions: Be careful of traffic and park well off the road. The tailings piles are quite steep; do not climb very high.

Special attractions: Gila Hot Springs Pools and Campground can be found along the West Fork of the Gila River. Gila Cliff Dwellings National Monument has a fine display of local minerals. Silver City has lots of downtown galleries and is also home to the Royal Scepter Museum and Rock Shop. Tyrone Copper Mine has a display and observation area on Tyrone Thomas Road (Forest Road 136). Travel about 11.7 miles south on Highway 90 from its junction with Broadway in Silver City. Turn right (west) onto Tyrone Thomas Road (FR 136). The observation deck can be seen when you turn.

Finding the site: This area is located between Fierro and Hanover in the Santa Rita Mining District east of Silver City. In Silver City from the junction of Highway 90 and U.S. Highway 180, go east out on US 180 to Highway 152 and turn left (northeast). Travel 4.6 miles on Highway 152, then turn left (north) on Highway 356. The dumps along the road start almost immediately on the left.

Rockhounding

This is one of the very productive mines in the area. It is a patented claim, but the dumps come down to the right-of-way and collecting is allowed along the road. The GPS coordinates are for a decent parking area on the right. Good collecting can be found all the way to the gate, which is about 3 miles from where you turn onto Highway 356. We found chalcopyrite, magnetite, azurite, galena, hematite, chrysacolla, quartz, and calcite, while others have reported sphalerite, malachite, chalcosite, and cuprite.

Look especially for the lime green chrysacolla, which resembles serpentine. It cuts and polishes well if you can locate a solid piece. Some cuttable copper ores and hematite can also be found.

Rabb Canyon

Land type: Mountainous forest.
Best time of year: June through October.
Land manager: Gila National Forest.
Material: Moonstone.
Tools: Geological hammer.
Vehicle: Any.
Precautions and restrictions: Be sure you are in good enough condition to make this hike. Bears and cougars are in the area, so take the proper precautions. Do not trespass on claims.
Special attractions: Gila Hot Springs Pools and Campground can be found along the West Fork of the Gila River. Gila Cliff Dwellings National Monument has a fine display of local minerals. Silver City has lots of downtown galleries and is also home to the Royal Scepter Museum and Rock Shop. Tyrone Copper Mine has a display and observation area on Tyrone Thomas Road (Forest Road 136). Travel about 11.7 miles south on Highway 90 from its junction with Broadway in Silver City. Turn right (west) onto Tyrone Thomas Road (FR 136). The observation deck can be seen when you turn.
Finding the site: We did not get to this area because of heavy snow. This area may be under claim now, so check for current information. There have been reports of alluvial pieces being found, and there may be other deposits nearby. The directions and rockhounding description below were written by Merrill O. Murphy and appeared in the *Newsletter of the New Mexico Faceters Guild.*

From Truth or Consequences, take Interstate 25 south about 10 miles to exit 63 and turn west on Highway 152. Continue west, more or less, through Hillsboro and Kingston. Stay on Highway 152, climbing steeply over Emory Pass. Check your odometer at the top, then drive carefully down the west side of the pass for about 10 miles. At this point the road flattens momentarily before leaving the valley and climbs to the top of a low hillside. Slow down and as the road goes gently downward, watch carefully on your right for an opening in the trees with a livestock corral at the back of the open space. Drive about 50 feet toward the corral, then turn west (left) and continue 75 feet. Stop and examine the dirt road leading west into a gully to make sure your vehicle has enough clearance to continue. If not, park in the clearing. Walk or drive down this primitive road to a shallow valley (Noonday Canyon), where the road turns north and crosses a shallow ford. (There may be a trickle of water here.) Cross and continue beside an old fence line until you reach another clearing, a distance of about 200 yards. There is an east–west fence and gate just beyond the clearing. This clearing is the trailhead. If you have driven in, pull off the road and park here.

Climb the ridge on the west of the clearing, going about 20 to 30 degrees north of west. A distinct trail should be visible near the top of the ridge. This trail runs north a short distance to a second gate in the east–west fence. After reaching this second gate, the trail angles and goes nearly west across the ridge. If, however, you have found no trail and no gate at the top of the ridge, go back to the trailhead and follow the dirt road north no more than 100 yards to the east–west fence. Then walk west up the fence line until you reach the second gate near the top of the ridge. From this ridgetop gate, the trail leads gently up and down a few hundred yards before diving abruptly into Rabb Canyon.

Rockhounding

Go up Rabb Canyon, where you should find pools of water in the canyon bottom. If you look closely, you will see bright blue flashes from tiny moonstones in the water. The canyon turns to the west a short distance upstream, and the water disappears in the sand. Continue up Rabb Canyon until you see a shallow arroyo on your right. Cross the arroyo (there may be a trickle of water in it) and take a trail leading northwest. This trail goes only a short distance before crossing the arroyo. Follow the trail paralleling the arroyo, keeping it no more than 50 feet to your left. After about a quarter mile, the indistinct trail will reach a livestock corral. Turn left and walk to the arroyo bank. About a half truckload of white feldspar should be visible on the far side. It is opaque, cracked, and shows little adularescence. It is part of a pegmatite that follows a fissure down from the main deposit.

Get down in the arroyo and go up it no more than 30 yards to a very indistinct gulch that joins the main arroyo from the west. This gulch leads to the moonstone site. Follow it more or less to the west. The banks will begin to steepen. Watch for a trail angling up the right-hand bank. This trail will climb out to a bowl-like little mesa measuring no more than two or three acres. When you climb out of the gulch, continue a short distance west. You should see the remains of a tiny cabin. Blue moonstone is scattered on the sands between the remains and the lower edge of a sharp ridge. Silver-white moonstone comes from the north part of the bowl. Shallow prospects are visible here and there along the west and north edges of the bowl. You will find lots of fine but very small bits of blue moonstone. The white moonstone will be in larger pieces. Few pieces of either will yield good cut stones.

Kingston

Land type: High desert.

Best time of year: April through October.

Land manager: New Mexico Department of Transportation.

Material: Quartz crystals.

Tools: Geological hammer, small shovel, gads, sledgehammer, and chisels.

Vehicle: Any.

Special attractions: Gila Hot Springs Pools and Campground can be found along the West Fork of the Gila River. Gila Cliff Dwellings National Monument has a fine display of local minerals. Silver City has lots of downtown galleries and is also home to the Royal Scepter Museum and Rock Shop. Tyrone Copper Mine has a display and observation area on Tyrone Thomas Road (Forest Road 136). Travel about 11.7 miles south on Highway 90 from its junction with Broadway in Silver City. Turn right (west) onto Tyrone Thomas Road (FR 136). The observation deck can be seen when you turn.

Finding the site: From the junction of Highways 152 and 27 in Hillsboro, drive about 9 miles west on Highway 152 to Kingston. Once in town keep to the right and leave the highway on an unnamed road, then in about 0.2 mile turn right (north). Continue about another 0.7 mile to a gate and park.

Rockhounding

This is one of the locations we never got to, again because of snow. The information we have was gathered from others who have been there.

Quartz crystals of all shapes can be found at this site. Some are singly terminated, but a few doubles as well as specters are available for those who are persistent. Rockhounds can either sift through the loose dirt or use their heavy equipment to split the rhyolite to look for pockets. This is hard work but worth the effort.

Chloride Mine

Land type: Mountainous forest.
GPS: N33° 20' 23" / W107° 42' 24".
Elevation: 6,409 feet.
Best time of year: All year.
Land manager: Gila National Forest.
Material: Chrysacolla, pyrite, chalcopyrite, crystal pockets, bornite, azurite, hematite, barite, galena, calcite, amethyst, malachite, chlorargyrite, and argentite.
Tools: Various size shovels, geological hammer, and spray bottle.
Vehicle: Four-wheel drive, or any vehicle with about a 2-mile hike.
Precautions and restrictions: Beware of open shafts in the area. It may be snow-covered in winter, and during rainy periods the canyon may be flooded and impassable.
Special attractions: Truth or Consequences (T or C) has a number of commercial hot spring facilities. It sure feels good to have a soak after a day of rockhounding. Elephant Butte Lake is located east of T or C and offers good

Crystal pockets at the Chloride Mine.

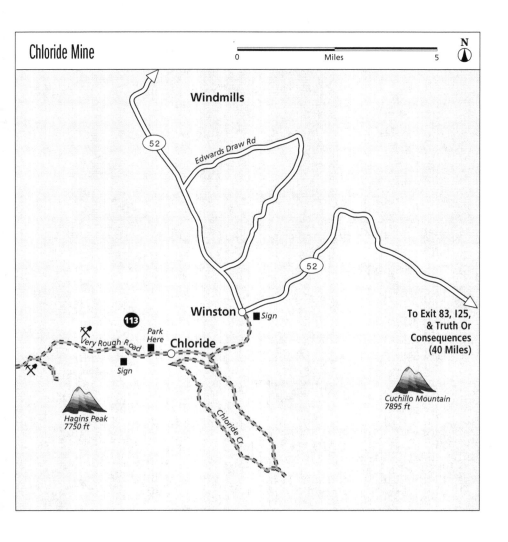

0   Miles   5

N

Windmills

52

Edwards Draw Rd

52

Winston ■ *Sign*

113

Park Here

Very Rough Road   **Chloride**

Sign

To Exit 83, 125, & Truth Or Consequences (40 Miles)

Cuchillo Mountain 7895 ft

Chloride Cr

Hagins Peak 7750 ft

fishing and nice hikes. The Mineral Museum of the New Mexico Bureau of Mines and Mineral Resources in Socorro is well worth a visit.

Finding the site: The chloride mines are located about 45 miles northwest of Truth or Consequences and just west of the small town of Chloride. From Truth or Consequences, take Interstate 25 north to exit 83 and continue on Highway 52 to Winston. Turn left (south) at the sign to Chloride. From this junction, drive 2.9 miles on an unnamed road through Winston and to the western edge of Chloride. Continue as the road makes a sharp left and enters a canyon. Here you need to either park or continue with a four-wheel-drive vehicle, as the road becomes rough and crosses Mineral and Chloride Creeks numerous times. After the road makes the sharp left, you can drive 0.5 mile to another parking area. We parked here since the road became even rougher. From the second parking area, walk 0.4 mile to the Gila National Forest sign, then continue past the sign another 0.9 mile to the first tailings piles. The GPS coordinates were taken at this spot.

Rockhounding

The directions are to the first pile of tailings encountered, but many more can be found farther up the road. We found chrysacolla, pyrite, chalcopyrite, crystal pockets, bornite, azurite, hematite, barite, galena, calcite, and amethyst just by walking around and exploring the shallow digging at the first tailings mound, and others have reported malachite, chlorargyrite, and argentite at this site. Better specimens can be found by digging deeper and spending more time in the area.

Truth or Consequences

Land type: Rocky, mountainous, high desert.

GPS: Site A: N33° 08' 38" / W107° 17' 05". Site B: N33° 08' 38" / W107° 16' 59".

Elevation: Site A: 4,592 feet. Site B: 4,563 feet.

Best time of year: All year.

Land manager: Bureau of Land Management, Las Cruces District.

Material: Picture rock (a rhyolite also known as candy rock) and marine fossils, including brachiopods, crinoid stems, and bivalves.

Tools: Chisels, sledgehammer, geological hammer, gads, and goggles.

Vehicle: Four-wheel drive.

Precautions and restrictions: Though it is tempting, know your limits and carry out only what is reasonable. This is heavy stuff.

Special attractions: Truth or Consequences (T or C) has a number of commercial hot spring facilities. It sure feels good to have a soak after a day of rockhounding. Elephant Butte Lake is located east of T or C and offers good fishing and nice hikes.

Finding the site: This area is located just west of Truth or Consequences. Take exit 79 off Interstate 25 onto Business I-25 south. Turn right onto Marie Street for 0.5 mile, then turn right onto Kopra. Follow Kopra 0.4 mile and pass under I-25. Make the first left after the underpass and travel 0.5 mile to the next left. Here the road narrows; go 0.2 mile and turn right. Climb a number of steep up-and-down hills as the road winds away from the highway. After 0.6 mile take the right fork toward the satellite dishes for another 0.3 mile. Drive past the dishes and park on the left before the wires pass over the road. Hike up the left fork. If you have a rugged vehicle, it may be possible to drive the third of a mile to the picture rock and fossil sites.

Rockhounding

After walking up the steep road, a few washes will be encountered; this is site A. The first wash has a few fossils, but most come from the second. Dig through the loose stuff on the sides and in the bottom of the washes to find casts and molds. Additional material can be located by splitting the rocks on the way up the trail.

You can find colorful picture rock not far from Truth or Consequences.

Past the fossil site, about 0.3 mile from the parking area, is site B, where you can find the picture rock. You will see big boulders and diggings off to the right (north) of the road. Small pieces of rhyolite will be scattered all over the terrain, and big boulders of the stuff can also be found along the trail. This material polishes well and makes beautiful jewelry and decorative pieces. The rugged road continues for about another 0.5 mile, where it ends at the top of the hill. There you can find more colorful pieces of picture rock.

At the time of this writing, it appears there may be claims in the area. Check with the Sierra County Clerk to see if these are valid. Even so, the same picture rock can be found all through the hills and vales of this area. It just may take a bit of splitting to determine which pieces are best.

Jornada Lakes

Land type: Desert.
GPS: N33° 06' 42" / W107° 02' 01".
Elevation: 4,732 feet.
Best time of year: October through April.
Land manager: Bureau of Land Management, Las Cruces District.
Material: Agatized wood and jasper.
Tools: Spray bottle and geological hammer.
Vehicle: Any.
Precautions and restrictions: This is a very remote site. Make sure that you have enough fuel and your vehicle is in good working order, and always carry plenty of water. This place gets really hot in summer.
Special attractions: Truth or Consequences (T or C) has a number of commercial hot spring facilities. It sure feels good to have a soak after a day of rockhounding. Elephant Butte Lake is located east of T or C and offers good fishing and nice hikes.
Finding the site: There are good collecting areas southeast of Truth or Consequences along County Road A13. Take exit 79 off Interstate 25 to Business I-25 south. Turn left (east) onto Highway 51 and continue 16 miles, then turn right (south) in Engle onto CR A13, a paved road that soon becomes gravel. The GPS coordinates were taken at 4.5 miles.

Rockhounding

Starting about 3 or 4 miles south of Engle, well-agatized pieces of wood can be found on both sides of the road. The collecting area continues for another 3 to 4 miles. Though most pieces are small and only suitable for tumbling, there are enough larger ones for those who like to cut their own cabochons. The GPS coordinates only represent one collecting area.

Engle

Land type: Desert.

GPS: N32° 59' 28"/ W107° 00' 30".

Elevation: 4,657 feet.

Best time of year: October through April.

Land manager: Bureau of Land Management, Las Cruces District.

Material: Carnelian, jasper, agate, and petrified wood.

Tools: Spray bottle, geological hammer, and small shovel.

Vehicle: Any vehicle is OK, except when the road is wet.

Precautions and restrictions: This is a very remote site. Make sure that you have enough fuel and your vehicle is in good working order, and always carry plenty of water.

Special attractions: Truth or Consequences (T or C) has a number of commercial hot spring facilities. It sure feels good to have a soak after a day of rockhounding. Elephant Butte Lake is located east of T or C and offers good fishing and nice hikes.

Finding the site: This area is famous for the beautiful carnelian pieces found in the washes and gullies at the foothills of the Caballo Mountains, southeast of Truth or Consequences. Take exit 79 off Interstate 25 and head south on Business I-25. Turn left (east) onto Highway 51 and continue 16 miles, then turn right (south) in Engle onto County Road A13, a paved road that soon turns to gravel. Continue 13 miles to the site of the old town Aleman. You will see a ranch house off to the left, some distance from the road. Continue a very short distance, then turn right (east) and pass through the gate (be sure to close it behind you). After you cross the railroad tracks, continue on this gravel road into the hills ahead. The collecting area starts at the beginning of the road and continues on into the far foothills of the Caballo Mountains.

Rockhounding

Carnelian has been collected here for a very long time; however, enough erosion takes place that new pieces are constantly being exposed. Most are small, but with persistence, cuttable chunks can be found. Some of the carnelian is simply clear red to amber, but other pieces are beautifully banded and make fantastic cabs.

You can start finding carnelian at the gate, where the GPS coordinates were taken; the bed continues for about 3 miles. It is best to walk away from the road, as the areas close to it are the first to be picked over.

Point of Rocks

Land type: High desert.
GPS: N32° 49' 09" / W107° 01' 16".
Elevation: 4,456 feet.
Best time of year: All year.
Land manager: Bureau of Land Management, Las Cruces District.
Material: Banded chalcedony, chalcedony roses, moss agate, druzy quartz, and petrified wood.
Tools: Geological hammer and small shovel.
Vehicle: Any vehicle will do most of the time, but four-wheel drive is necessary when the road is wet.
Precautions and restrictions: This is a very remote area, so be sure that your vehicle is in good working order and that you carry extra water.
Special attractions: Truth or Consequences (T or C) has a number of commercial hot spring facilities. Elephant Butte Lake is located east of T or C and offers good fishing and nice hikes.
Finding the site: This site is located in the foothills of Point of Rocks, about 15 miles northeast of the town of Rincon. From Interstate 25, just south of Rincon, take exit 32 and follow County Road G72 northwest toward Engle. This soon becomes County Road 72. You will see Point of Rocks in the distance to the northeast. Begin clocking your mileage when you reach the junction with County Road 75. Continue on CR 72 and in 5 miles you will see rough tracks leading to the east in the direction of Point of Rocks. Park here.

Rockhounding

Heading toward the foothills of the mountains to the east, one can pick up a variety of agate. Carefully explore the ground beneath you as you hike toward the hills. Many of the agates are partly embedded in the soft soil. Inspect each piece thoroughly, and be sure to chip likely suspects.

We found numerous small chalcedony roses, some banded and others with red and pink inclusions and a druzy overlay. As we hiked toward the hills, we found larger pieces, some of which were big enough to cut into cabs. We also found samples of petrified wood and one large chunk of multicolored moss agate. Nothing is overly abundant, but a good amount can be collected with persistence.

The GPS coordinates are for the first place we found a piece of agate. We then walked east toward the hills and found a lot more.

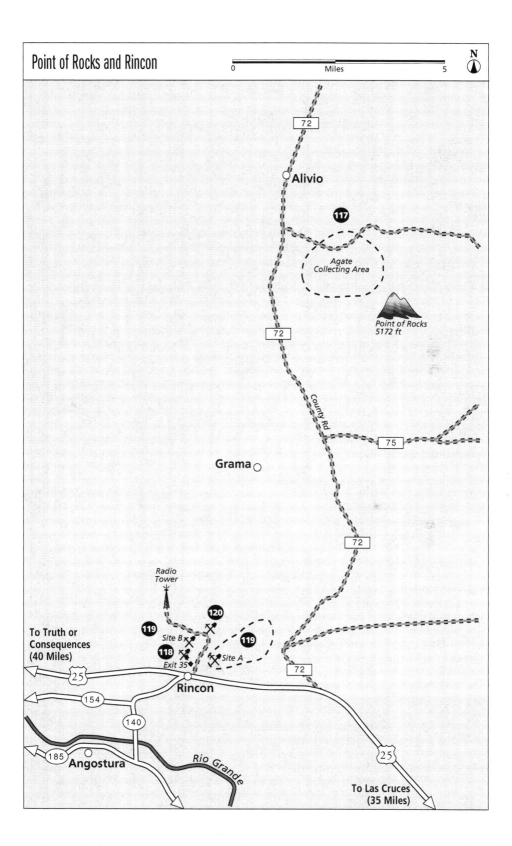

Point of Rocks and Rincon

Rincon Barite Quarry

See map on page 191.
Land type: Mountainous desert.
GPS: N32° 40' 50" / W107° 03' 30".
Elevation: 4,214 feet.
Best time of year: All year.
Land manager: Bureau of Land Management, Las Cruces District.
Material: Barite crystals, agate, and jasper.
Tools: Geological hammer, chisels, gads, sledgehammer, goggles, and crowbar.
Vehicle: High-clearance four-wheel drive, or any vehicle with a 0.4-mile hike.
Precautions and restrictions: Use extreme caution around the walls of the quarry, and watch for falling rocks. Always wear goggles when hammering or chiseling. Take a look at the road to the quarry to determine if your vehicle can make it, as it is very difficult to turn around once you make the commitment to proceed.
Special attractions: Caballo Lake State Park offers camping, fishing, boating, and geological exploration. In Las Cruces, check out the Las Cruces Museum of Natural History and the Branigan Cultural Center.
Finding the site: From Interstate 25, take exit 35 at Rincon and drive northeast 0.1 mile on the road that heads toward the tower. You will see a road off to the left (north) and the quarry in the distance. Turn up this road, drive 0.4 mile, and park unless you are absolutely sure your vehicle can make it up the very rough road to the quarry.

Rockhounding

Some fine clusters of barite crystals can be found here. They make beautiful display pieces. You can probably find some by simply examining the quarry rocks. If this doesn't work, hammering and chiseling are in order. We also found agate and jasper at this site.

Rincon Jasper and Agate

See map on page 191.

Land type: Mountainous desert.

GPS: Site A: N32° 40' 43" / W107° 03' 17". Site B: N32° 41' 19" / W107° 03' 34".

Elevation: Site A: 4,101 feet. Site B: 6,150 feet.

Best time of year: All year.

Land manager: Bureau of Land Management, Las Cruces District.

Material: Agate, crystals, and jasper.

Tools: Geological hammer, spray bottle, and small shovel.

Vehicle: Any vehicle will do until the last half mile, at which point four-wheel drive is necessary unless you walk the remaining distance.

Precautions and restrictions: Park well off the road.

Special attractions: Caballo Lake State Park offers camping, fishing, boating, and geological exploration. In Las Cruces, check out the Las Cruces Museum of Natural History and the Branigan Cultural Center.

Finding the site: From Interstate 15, take exit 35 at Rincon and drive northeast 0.1 mile on the road that heads toward the tower. The mounds of dirt on the right (south) is site A. Drive another 1.5 miles up the mountain to site B.

Rockhounding

As you are driving in, you will notice a few mounds on the right (south). These hold many fine but small pieces of agate and jasper. Larger pieces of nice jasper can be picked up at site B.

Rincon Fossils

See map on page 191.

Land type: Mountainous desert.

Best time of year: March through November.

Land manager: Bureau of Land Management, Las Cruces District.

Material: Marine fossils, chalcedony, and agate.

Tools: Geological hammer, small shovel, goggles, pick, sledgehammer, chisels, and gads.

Vehicle: Any vehicle is OK unless it has rained recently, in which case four-wheel drive is needed.

Precautions and restrictions: The parking area seems to be a place where some people bring their dead animals. We saw a cow, a couple of sheep, a dog, and a few unidentified decomposing critters. We were there in the winter and can only imagine how unpleasant this might be in summer. Always wear goggles chiseling.

Special attractions: Caballo Lake State Park offers camping, fishing, boating, and geological exploration. In Las Cruces, check out the Las Cruces Museum of Natural History and the Branigan Cultural Center.

Finding the site: From Interstate 25, take exit at Rincon and drive northeast 1.1 miles on the road that heads toward the tower. You'll see a pull-off on the right (south) just before the road becomes very steep.

Rockhounding

Some nice pieces of coral can be extracted here. You can pick up what others left behind or do your own chiseling.

Border Chalcedony

Land type: High desert.

Best time of year: November through April.

Land manager: Bureau of Land Management, Las Cruces District.

Material: Chalcedony roses, black chalcedony roses, moss agate, and pink and lavender banded agate.

Tools: Geological hammer and spray bottle.

Vehicle: The road can be rough and washboardy but is usually passable with any vehicle.

Precautions and restrictions: This is a very remote site, so be sure that your vehicle is in good shape and you have enough fuel and water. We have been told that snakes are very common in this area during the warm months. It can get very hot here in summer and could be snow-covered during winter.

Special attractions: Shakespeare Ghost Town, just outside of Lordsburg, is a theme park built around the old mining town of Shakespeare. There are hot springs across the border in Safford, Arizona.

Finding the site: From the junction of U.S. Highway 70 and Highway 90 in Lordsburg, drive 15 miles west on US 70 to an unnamed road on the left (west) at milepost 13. Turn onto this road and go 7 miles. After crossing railroad tracks and a cattle guard in quick succession, proceed another 1.8 miles to a second cattle guard. Continue 2.9 miles to a gate with a no trespassing sign. Park before the gate.

Rockhounding

This location has been famous for a long time for the quality of its agates and nodules; however, there may be some land ownership issues. Upon reaching the last gate, a large no trespassing sign has been posted, but there is a question as to whether this applies to the road or just the land off the road. In any case, if you decide to not drive past the sign, good-quality material can be found in the desert for about a mile before reaching the gate. This is not the pink banded agate that could be dug farther along the road, but rather beautiful black chalcedony roses that, when held up to the light, glow a handsome amber color. These make fine jewelry and are real conversation pieces. Nice moss and banded agate can also be picked up here. The technique is to walk slowly and cover as much ground as possible. The gems will easily be spotted.

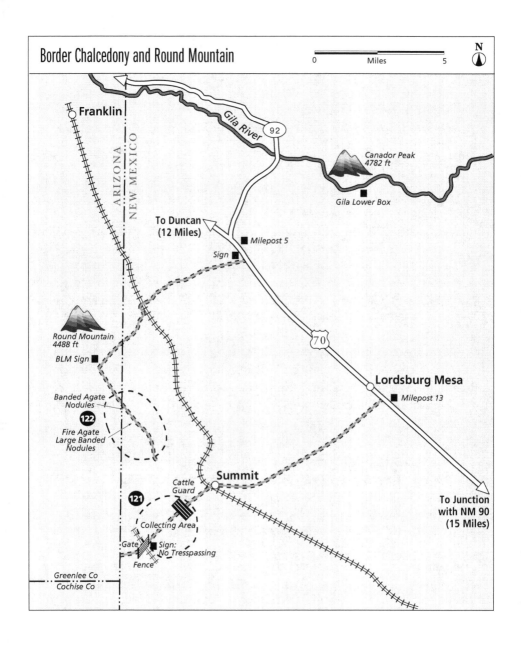

Border Chalcedony and Round Mountain

Round Mountain

See map on page 196.

Land type: High desert.

GPS: N32° 30' 24" / W109° 03' 18".

Elevation: 4,147 feet.

Best time of year: November through April.

Land manager: Bureau of Land Management, Las Cruces District.

Material: Fire agate, banded agate, moss agate, chalcedony roses, crystal nodules, and jasper.

Tools: Geological hammer and spray bottle.

Vehicle: Any vehicle is OK unless it has rained recently, in which case four-wheel drive is needed.

Precautions and restrictions: This is a very remote site, so be sure that your vehicle is in good shape and you have enough fuel and water. We have been told that snakes are very common in the area during the warm months. It can be very hot here in summer.

Special attractions: Shakespeare Ghost Town, just outside of Lordsburg, is a theme park built around the old mining town of Shakespeare. There are hot springs in Safford, Arizona.

Finding the site: This site covers an area on both sides of the New Mexico–Arizona state line northwest of Lordsburg, near the Arizona town of Duncan. From the junction of U.S. Highway 70 and Highway 90 in Lordsburg, go 23.5 miles west on US 70 toward Duncan. At 0.6 mile before milepost 5 (as measured from the Arizona border), turn left on an unnamed road and go over a cattle guard by a sign that reads LAZY B RANCH. Continue 6.8 miles to a BLM sign that says ROUND MOUNTAIN ROCKHOUNDING AREA and turn left onto another dirt road. The collecting area starts at about 1.5 miles and continues all the way to the base of Round Mountain.

Rockhounding

The collecting area here is extensive, and the material changes with each stop along the road. In one area you might find crystal nodules, but stop another few hundred yards farther, and chalcedony roses with red areas will be evident. Any pieces that contain red areas might be the precious fire agate. Go on a sunny day and spray each suspect piece with water. You may want to break some pieces to see what treasures can be found inside. The GPS coordinates are for the first area where we found fire.

Fuller Road Chalcedony

Land type: High desert.

GPS: N32° 36' 53" / W108° 48' 33".

Elevation: 4,304 feet.

Best time of year: October through May.

Land manager: Bureau of Land Management, Las Cruces District.

Material: Chalcedony roses and moss agate.

Tools: Geological hammer, spray bottle, and small shovel.

Vehicle: Any vehicle will do to the unmarked road, at which point four-wheel drive is necessary unless you walk the remaining distance.

Precautions and restrictions: This is a very remote site, so be sure that your vehicle is in good shape and you have enough fuel and water. We have been told that snakes are very common in the area during the warm months. It can get very hot here in summer.

Special attractions: Shakespeare Ghost Town, just outside of Lordsburg, is a theme park built around the old mining town of Shakespeare. There are hot springs across the border in Safford, Arizona.

Finding the site: From the junction of U.S. Highway 70 and Highway 90 in Lordsburg, travel northwest on US 70 for 19.5 miles to Fuller Road. Turn right (east) and drive 7.5 miles on Fuller, then turn left (north) onto an unmarked gravel road. The collecting area starts at 1 mile and continues for at least 2 or 3 more miles.

Rockhounding

We found this site by accident, having gotten lost looking for another. Chalcedony roses from ½ inch to 5 inches across can be found throughout the collecting area. Some are covered with very pretty druzy quartz and would make beautiful jewelry pieces after just a little cleaning. A few of the flowers have areas of red. Though we did not find any, this location might yield some fire agate for those ambitious enough to take the time to give it a thorough going over. We also may not have found fire because the day was cloudy. Some nice moss agate can also be picked up at this location.

Pine Canyon

See map on page 177.

Land type: Mountainous forest.

GPS: N32° 37' 11" / W108° 29' 14".

Elevation: 6,585 feet.

Best time of year: April through October.

Land manager: Gila National Forest.

Material: Fluorite and quartz.

Tools: Geological hammer, spray bottle and bucket of water, and small shovel.

Vehicle: Any vehicle is OK, unless the roads are snowy and/or icy.

Precautions and restrictions: This area is quite remote, so make sure that your vehicle is in proper working order and carry enough fuel and water. Snow and ice can be a problem in winter.

Special attractions: Gila Hot Springs Pools and Campground can be found along the West Fork of the Gila River. Gila Cliff Dwellings National Monument has a fine display of local minerals. Silver City has lots of downtown galleries and is also home to the Royal Scepter Museum and Rock Shop. Tyrone Copper Mine has a display and observation area on Tyrone Thomas Road (Forest Road 136). Travel about 11.7 miles south on Highway 90 from its junction with Broadway in Silver City. Turn right (west) onto Tyrone Thomas Road (FR 136). The observation deck can be seen when you turn.

Finding the site: Pine Canyon is located about 15 miles southwest of Silver City. From the junction of Highway 90 and Broadway in Silver City, go 11.7 miles south on Highway 90 to Forest Road 136 and turn right (east). Drive past the Tyrone Mine tailings on the right, following FR 136 for 9.8 miles to its junction with Forest Road 851. Here FR 136 turns sharply to the left; continue on FR 136 for 0.5 mile, at which point you will see Forest Road 4250X on the right. Pass this road and take the next right, which is only a few feet from the first. This is a very rough road, even for four-wheel-drive vehicles, so park near the bottom. Walk uphill several hundred yards, then turn right onto Forest Road 4250Z and follow it several hundred yards to its end at a circle. To the left you will see a low wall of rocks. Climb past this and follow the trail a short way to the diggings.

Rockhounding

Fine clusters of fluorite cubes, many coated with druzy quartz crystals, are found in this area. The colors range from white and clear to deep green, purple, lavender, and even an occasional royal blue. We also found massive white fluorite with areas of all of the above colors. This cuts and polishes into very attractive cabs and other decorative pieces. Some of the fluorite is clear enough for faceting.

The diggings are small and can be easily missed, so be observant of ground disturbances when you are in the area. After a rainfall it is easy to find small colorful pieces scattered on the ground, but to obtain the finest and largest specimens, you have to dig. Carefully wash and inspect any suspect pieces. This location has been under claim for many years, but the owners have allowed prospecting with hand tools at one's own risk. Check to determine the current status.

If you're feeling energetic, go back to the initial rough road but instead of going back to your vehicle, hike up the steep hill to the top (about 0.25 mile), where you will have an incredible 360-degree view of the surrounding national forest as it extends into the high desert. On a clear day it is well worth the hike.

Highway 90 Dendrites

Land type: Low hills, high desert.
GPS: N32° 35' 06" / W108° 20' 52".
Elevation: 5,975 feet.
Best time of year: All year.
Material: Dendritic limestone and chalcedony.
Tools: Geological hammer, screwdriver, sledgehammer, chisels, goggles, and gads.
Vehicle: Any.
Precautions and restrictions: Park well off the road, and be careful of loose rock falling from above. Always wear goggles when hammering or chiseling.
Special attractions: Gila Hot Springs Pools and Campground can be found along the West Fork of the Gila River. Gila Cliff Dwellings National Monument has a fine display of local minerals. Silver City has lots of downtown galleries and is also home to the Royal Scepter Museum and Rock Shop. Tyrone Copper Mine has a display and observation area on Tyrone Thomas Road (Forest Road 136). Travel about 11.7 miles south on Highway 90 from its junction

You will find a good source of dendritic limestone on Highway 90 south of Silver City.

with Broadway in Silver City. Turn right (west) onto Tyrone Thomas Road (FR 136). The observation deck can be seen when you turn.

Finding the site: From the junction of Highway 90 and Broadway in Silver City, head southwest on Highway 90 for 14.4 miles. As a landmark, before reaching the area you will pass Armyo Road. The material is in a large road cut on the left. From Lordsburg, it is immediately before milepost 28 on the right.

Rockhounding

This site is located in a road cut and is actually a parking area off the road. The limestone is bright white, and the dendrites are black. Dendrites are formed when a magnesium compound percolates through the ground and is deposited onto the rock. They take the form of ferns and/or other leafy plants. When you find the areas of the road cut that contain this material, it will be obvious. Take the nicest pieces that are exposed. To locate other planes of dendrites, you can hammer, chisel, or pry open the rocks with a screwdriver. The surface of this material is quite smooth. Do not grind it with a coarse wheel or you may lose the patterns. A 600 grit or just a polish will do. Some are handsome enough that no grinding is necessary—simply shape them. These pieces make nice belt buckles and bolos, and some of the finely patterned ones can be used for pendants.

Gold Hill

Land type: High desert.
GPS: N32° 25' 50" / W108° 32' 07".
Elevation: 5,774 feet.
Best time of year: October through May.
Land manager: Bureau of Land Management, Las Cruces District.
Material: Apricot quartz, white quartz, feldspar, and an unidentified green rock.
Tools: Geological hammer and shovel.
Vehicle: High-clearance four-wheel drive.
Precautions and restrictions: This is a very remote area, so be sure that your vehicle is in good working order and you have enough fuel and water. It would be a long walk out of the site back to Highway 90. Think about poisonous critters during the warm months.
Special attractions: There is an excellent view of Lordsburg on Highway 90 at 4.8 miles. Gila Hot Springs Pools and Campground can be found along the West Fork of the Gila River. Gila Cliff Dwellings National Monument has a fine display of local minerals. Silver City has lots of downtown galleries and is also home to the Royal Scepter Museum and Rock Shop. Tyrone Copper Mine has a display and observation area on Tyrone Thomas Road (Forest Road 136). Travel about 11.7 miles south on Highway 90 from its junction with Broadway in Silver City. Turn right (west) onto Tyrone Thomas Road (FR 136). The observation deck can be seen when you turn.
Finding the site: From the junction of U.S. Highway 70 and Highway 90 in Lordsburg, go 8 miles northeast on Highway 90 and turn right (east) onto gravel Forest Road 841. Continue for 1 mile and cross a cattle guard. After another 1.5 miles you will see a road on the right (south) leading to a mine dump. Continue on FR 841 another 0.8 mile to a Y. The left road has a sign that reads ROAD CLOSED TO THRU TRAFFIC. Bear right over a very hilly, windy, and rough road. At 0.9 mile pass through a gate (be sure to close it behind you) and continue for 0.8 mile. At that point you are at the start of the mining district.

Rockhounding

We found this site by accident while looking for a few old mines that were supposed to be in the area's mountains. We never located the old diggings, but found instead a very unique quartz. Apricot quartz is truly that color.

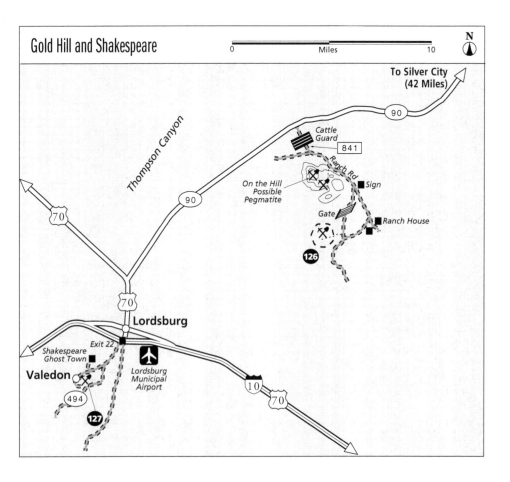

This material cuts and polishes well and makes beautiful cabs. One piece that we found actually has an unfractured clear area that might be good enough to facet, but it is questionable whether the color would show through in that form. A pretty green rock, as yet unidentified but probably containing some epidote, was also ambient at this location. This polishes well too.

Though we did not find the mines, it may pay to spend a few days searching the area. At times, locations that are difficult to uncover contain the most interesting stuff.

Shakespeare

See map on page 204.
Land type: Desert.
GPS: N32° 19' 05" / W108° 44' 29".
Elevation: 4,587 feet.
Best time of year: November through April.
Land manager: Bureau of Land Management, Las Cruces District.
Material: Chrysacolla, bornite, azurite, malachite, calcite, quartz crystals, hematite, linarite, and galena.
Tools: Geological hammer and spray bottle.
Vehicle: Any.
Precautions and restrictions: We have been told that snakes are very common in this area during the warm months. Beware of open abandoned mining pits. It can get very hot here in summer.
Special attractions: Shakespeare Ghost Town is a theme park built around the old mining town of Shakespeare.

Looking for copper ores at the dumps above Shakespeare.

Finding the site: From Interstate 10 in Lordsburg, go 1.3 miles south on Highway 494. Turn right (west) on an unmarked road and drive 0.7 mile to a fork. The right-hand turn leads to Shakespeare Ghost Town in 0.3 mile. The dump sites are located 0.5 mile up the left fork, on the left side of the road. Park and walk up the hill to the huge tailings piles.

Rockhounding

At this site we found chrysacolla, bornite, azurite, malachite, calcite, quartz crystals, and hematite, while others have reported linarite and galena. The tailings dumps are extensive. It is not too difficult to find lots of "color," and nice pieces can be found with diligence.

Cookes Peak

Land type: Rocky high desert.

GPS: Site A: N32° 27' 21" / W107° 44' 23". Site B: N32° 24' 37" / W107° 42' 50".

Elevation: Site A: 4,890 feet. Site B: 4,794 feet.

Best time of year: October through May.

Land manager: Bureau of Land Management, Las Cruces District.

Material: Carnelian, sard, sardonyx, jasper, agate, and quartz crystals.

Tools: Geological hammer and spray bottle.

Vehicle: Any vehicle will do if you stay on the main road, but side roads and washes may require four-wheel drive and high clearance. In wet weather, however, all bets are off!

Precautions and restrictions: This area is relatively remote, so be sure that your vehicle is in good working condition and you have plenty of fuel. It is generally very hot in the summer and even the winter months can sometimes be quite hot and dry, so be sure to carry plenty of water.

Special attractions: The Rockhound Roundup, one of the premier gem and mineral shows in the Southwest, usually takes place the first couple weeks of March. The show is put on by the Deming Gem and Mineral Society (see appendix D) at the Southwest New Mexico State Fairgrounds in Deming.

Finding the site: The Cookes Peak collecting area is located just northeast of Deming, and there are numerous roads leading to it. The sites described here are where we've been most successful. From Deming, drive north 1.2 miles on U.S. Highway 180, then turn right (northeast) onto Highway 26 and go 4.9 miles. Turn left (north) on Green Leaf Mine Road; you will immediately pass a large ranch house on the left. Proceed on this gravel road for 5.6 miles, pass a large block structure on the left, and continue 0.4 mile to a very large mine dump and structure on the left. In another 0.8 mile you will see a sandy road off to the left (west). This is the start of the site B collecting area, which continues for 2 miles on Green Leaf Mine Road. To get to site A, go 1.6 miles past site B and park anywhere that is safe. The site continues for about a mile or two down the road.

Rockhounding

Carnelian used to be plentiful here, but after many decades of collecting, it is now rather sparse. Looking for other agates is much more productive, but if it's

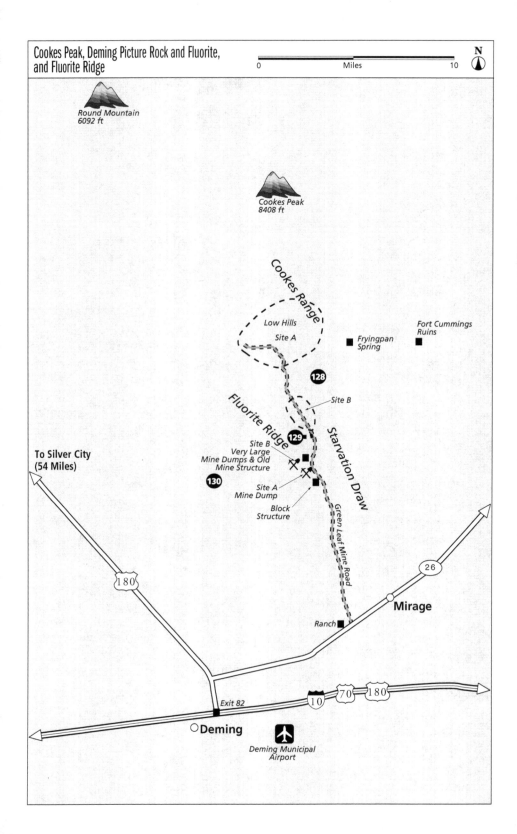

Round Mountain
6092 ft

Cookes Peak
8408 ft

Cookes Range

Low Hills
Site A

Fort Cummings
Ruins

Fryingpan
Spring

128

Site B

Fluorite Ridge

129

Starvation Draw

Site B
Very Large
Mine Dumps & Old
Mine Structure

To Silver City
(54 Miles)

130

Site A
Mine Dump

Block
Structure

Green Leaf Mine Road

26

180

Mirage

Ranch

Exit 82

10   70   180

Deming

Deming Municipal
Airport

Cookes Peak (in the distance) is a source of small pieces of carnelian.

carnelian you're after, site A would be a good bet. It is the most productive area that we found after many visits to the location. After parking at site A, hike toward the low hills in the distance. Walk slowly and carefully examine the ground, picking up any suspect stones. Have your spray bottle ready to clean off the desert dust. Also be on the lookout for nice pieces of agate and petrified wood. We have spent quite a few hours hiking this way, collecting a good handful of carnelian. We found more carnelian as we approached the hills—the closer the better. The pieces are generally very small, and you'd be lucky to find any over a half inch in size. If you want to stay close to the road, hike along it and examine the sides. Small pieces of carnelian often are uncovered as vehicles drive by.

Site B contains quite a bit of jasper, agate, sard, and petrified wood. Collecting at this site requires a willingness to hike and cover a large area. The site continues for about 2 miles, at which point the material becomes more sparse. Hike away from the road on both sides, and cover as much area as possible while carefully examining the ground. If your neck and back don't hurt at the end of the day from looking down, bending, and picking up likely suspects, then you haven't given it your personal best. After spending half a day hiking, we found sardonyx, colorful agates and rhyolite, and nice petrified wood, including a spectacular black piece with red inclusions. Site B's GPS coordinates were taken at the top of the rhyolite cliff, which is the approximate start of the agate collecting area.

Deming Picture Rock and Fluorite

See map on page 208.

Land type: Rocky high desert.

GPS: Site A: N32° 24' 37"/ W107° 42' 50". Site B: N32° 24' 36"/ W107° 42' 55".

Elevation: Site A: 4,794 feet. Site B: 4,830 feet.

Best time of year: October through April.

Land manager: Bureau of Land Management, Las Cruces District.

Material: Picture rock (also called candy rock) and fluorite.

Tools: Chisels, sledgehammer, goggles, gads, geological hammer, small shovel, and spray bottle.

Vehicle: Any vehicle will do up to last 0.4 mile on the sandy side road, at which point four-wheel drive is needed, or you can park and walk.

Precautions and restrictions: Beware of open mine pits in the area, and look out for falling rocks near cliffs. It can be very hot here in summer. Snakes and other poisonous things are around during the warm months.

Special attractions: The Rockhound Roundup, one of the premier gem and mineral shows in the Southwest, usually takes place the first couple weeks of March. The show is put on by the Deming Gem and Mineral Society (see appendix D) at the Southwest New Mexico State Fairgrounds in Deming.

Finding the site: This area is located northeast of Deming. From Deming, drive north 1.2 miles on U.S. Highway 180, then turn right (northeast) on Highway 26 and go 4.9 miles. Turn left (north) on Green Leaf Mine Road; you will immediately pass a large ranch house on the left. Proceed on this gravel road 5.6 miles, pass a large block structure, and continue 0.4 mile to a very large mine dump and structure on the left. In another 0.8 mile you will see a sandy road off to the left (west). Turn left and drive 0.4 mile to the parking/camping area.

Rockhounding

At the parking area you will be below a large cliff. (This is also a great camping spot—just don't stop too close to the cliff.) On the left-hand side, a trail leads up to the top of the crag. Small pieces of colorful patterned rhyolite can be collected along the trail and the hillside below it. Immediately at the top on the left is site A, which can be identified by big picture-rock workings. Find a few large boulders of the material at the base of the diggings.

Site B is a couple hundred feet farther up the trail. Here you will find diggings for nice fluorite cubes in all colors. Some are coated with druzy quartz.

Fluorite Ridge

See map on page 208.
Land type: Rocky high desert.
GPS: Site A: N32° 23' 39" / W107° 42' 24". Site B: N32° 23' 56" / W107° 42' 31".
Elevation: Site A: 4,621 feet. Site B: 4,702 feet.
Best time of year: November through May.
Land manager: Bureau of Land Management, Las Cruces District.
Material: Agate, jasper, petrified wood, quartz crystals, marine fossils, fluorite cubes, and purple, green, white, and clear massive fluorite.
Tools: Geological hammer, small shovel, pick, and bucket of water.
Vehicle: Any.
Precautions and restrictions: Beware of open abandoned mining pits in the area. It can be very hot here in summer. Snakes and other poisonous things are around during the warm months.
Special attractions: The Rockhound Roundup, one of the premier gem and mineral shows in the Southwest, usually takes place during the first couple weeks of March. The show is put on by the Deming Gem and Mineral Society (see appendix D) at the Southwest New Mexico State Fairgrounds in Deming.
Finding the site: This area is located northeast of Deming. From Deming, drive north 1.2 miles on U.S. Highway 180, then turn right (northeast) on Highway 26 and go 4.9 miles. Turn left (north) on Green Leaf Mine Road; you will immediately pass a large ranch house on the left. Proceed on this gravel road 5.6 miles to site A and another 0.4 mile to site B.

Rockhounding

At site A park at a pull-off on the left, walk to the small block structure straight ahead, and dig in the dumps behind it. We found cubes as well as massive fluorite in purple, green, white, and clear. A few fossils were also found here, and agates, rhyolite, and petrified wood are scattered throughout the area.

At site B all types of fluorite can be found by digging in the dumps on the left side of the road beside the mining structure. Walk around the hillside above it to find large rock specimens containing pockets of druzy quartz crystals as well as fluorite cubes. These make nice garden and display rocks, or they could be sliced and polished to use as colorful bookends.

Paradise

Land type: High desert.

GPS: Site A: N31° 56' 02" / W109° 11' 08". Site B: N31° 56' 12" / W109° 11' 29".

Elevation: Site A: 4,693 feet. Site B: 5,496 feet.

Best time of year: November through April.

Land manager: Coronado National Forest.

Material: Bornite, chalcopyrite, arginite, galena, quartz, calcite, azurite, chrysacolla, malachite, and an unidentified lavender and white rock.

Tools: Site A: Geological hammer and spray bottle. Site B: Geological hammer, chisels, sledgehammer, gads, goggles, and crowbar.

Vehicle: Any.

Precautions and restrictions: There are open pits in the area, so be very care-ful. Always wear goggles when chiseling—you want to save your eyes so that you can continue to admire all those beautiful minerals.

Special attractions: Chiricahua National Monument boasts some of the most unusual rock formations in North America, along with camping, hiking, and wildlife watching. Quaint and artsy shops can be found in the towns of Rodeo, New Mexico, and Portal, Arizona. Shakespeare Ghost Town, just outside of Lordsburg, is a theme park built around the old mining town of Shakespeare.

Finding the site: From Animas at the junction of Highways 338 and 9, take Highway 9 west to Highway 80. Go south on Highway 80 toward Rodeo for 3.4 miles, then west on Highway 533 toward Portal, Arizona. At 7.7 miles bear right onto Paradise Road, which is a graded dirt road. At 1.5 miles you will see a Forest Service sign on the left. Drive another 1.3 miles, where you will no-tice a very steep road going uphill to large mounds of tailings on the right (north). Park on the left (south) side at the parking/camping area and walk up about a quarter mile to site A. Site B is 0.1 mile farther on the right (north) side of the road. Park on the right and walk about a half mile to the diggings.

Rockhounding

This location is actually in Arizona, but the easiest access is through New Mex-ico. A steep but short hike up to site A will yield some beautiful specimens and even cutting material for those willing to put in some time. It is a great area for finding micromounts of copper minerals. We also found some wonderful azurite crystals on white calcite that make very handsome, though small, display pieces. Some of the bright white calcite contains areas of assorted copper, silver, and lead minerals such as bornite, azurite, chrysacolla, malachite, galena, chalcopyrite, and argentite, among others. Beautiful cabs resulted when this material was cut and polished.

Site B is the quartz crystal location. We found some as long as 1½ inches, but most are between ½ and ¾ inch. They have clear tips and are found lining pockets as clusters in a very hard lavender and white country rock. With diligence and hard work these cavities can be extracted and would make very nice display items. A few crystals can be found by digging and searching around areas where others had been chiseling. The pretty lavender and white rock polishes nicely and makes fine cabs and other decorative items like bookends.

San Simon Mine

Land type: High desert.

GPS: N32° 05' 21" / W108° 58' 03"

Elevation: 4,499 feet.

Best time of year: October through May.

Land manager: Bureau of Land Management, Las Cruces District.

Material: Azurite, chrysacolla, magnitite, garnet, beryl, calcite, quartz, and an unidentified flat crystal that might be a calcite pseudomorph of mica.

Tools: Geological hammer, small shovel, and spray bottle.

Vehicle: Any vehicle will do until the last 0.3 mile, at which point four-wheel drive or walking is necessary.

Precautions and restrictions: There are open pits and steep tailings piles in the area, so be careful.

Special attractions: Chiricahua National Monument boasts some of the most unusual rock formations in North America, along with camping, hiking, and wildlife watching. Quaint and artsy shops can be found in the towns of Rodeo, New Mexico, and Portal, Arizona. Shakespeare Ghost Town, just outside of Lordsburg, is a theme park built around the old mining town of Shakespeare.

Finding the site: The mine is about 15 miles southwest of Lordsburg. From Lordsburg, travel west on Interstate 10 to the Road Forks exit (exit 5), then go south on Highway 80 for 11.5 miles. Either park your vehicle here and walk, or turn left (east) onto tracks leading 0.3 mile up the hill to the tailings pile.

Rockhounding

Lots of color will be seen as you approach the tailings. We found good specimens as well as some cutting material. Though the latter is rather scarce, diligence will yield some. The desert around the mine is littered with chunks of white quartz, and there may be some pegmatites in the area. We did find a nice-size light green beryl crystal. Some garnet, including small but well-formed red crystals, were also apparent. Some of the dark country rock have veins of the various copper ores running through them. This takes a nice polish and makes some very pretty cabs.

Animas

Land type: High desert.

GPS: Site A: N31° 57' 47" / W108° 40' 31". Site B: N31° 57' 50" / W108° 39' 32".

Elevation: Site A: 4,474 feet. Site B: 4,430 feet.

Best time of year: November through April.

Land manager: Bureau of Land Management, Las Cruces District.

Material: Brown, blue, white, and red banded/swirled rhyolite; white agate; crystals; and an unidentified red/black ore.

Tools: Geological hammer and spray bottle.

Vehicle: Any.

Special attractions: Chiricahua National Monument boasts some of the most unusual rock formations in North America, along with camping, hiking, and wildlife watching. Quaint and artsy shops can be found in the towns of Rodeo, New Mexico, and Portal, Arizona. Shakespeare Ghost Town, just outside of Lordsburg, is a theme park built around the old mining town of Shakespeare. The Rockhound Roundup, one of the premier gem and mineral shows in the Southwest, usually takes place during the first couple weeks of March. The show is put on by the Deming Gem and Mineral Society (see appendix D) at the Southwest New Mexico State Fairgrounds in Deming.

Finding the site: This area is located about 25 miles south of Lordsburg. From Lordsburg, travel west on Interstate 10 to exit 11, then drive 23.4 miles on Highway 338 its junction with Highway 9 in Animas. Turn left (east) on Highway 9 and go 7.8 miles to site A. To get site B, drive another mile (8.8 miles total) and turn right (south) on a rough gravel road. Go 0.2 mile on this road and park before a wash.

Rockhounding

Some fine pieces of banded rhyolite can be found along the side of the road at site A. The colors range from white to red, blue, and brown and all the shades in between. Stop the car at the given mileage and start looking around. We found plenty of rhyolite without climbing over a fence, but a lot more was evident on the other side. Pay particular attention to the culvert under the road. Rhyolite polishes up into fine decorative pieces and cabs. (Some say that you have to use a leather buffer in the final step.) A few white agates can also be picked up at this location.

More agates are found at site B. Most are white in the form of roses, but some are coated with a very attractive druzy and are suitable for jewelry after just a bit of cleaning. We also found a nice piece of white plume agate and a few small chunks of moss agate.

Hachita

Land type: High desert.
GPS: N31° 56' 58" / W108° 25' 35".
Elevation: 4,696 feet.
Best time of year: October through April.
Land manager: Bureau of Land Management, Las Cruces District.
Material: Agate, jasper, and rhyolite.
Tools: Geological hammer and spray bottle.
Vehicle: Any vehicle will do, but four-wheel drive is recommended to drive the 0.4-mile dirt road.
Precautions and restrictions: It can get very hot here during the summer, so be sure to carry enough water. Locals told us that there are lots of snakes in the area. If you spend the night, make sure you park at least a quarter mile from the water hole.
Special attractions: Chiricahua National Monument boasts some of the most unusual rock formations in North America, along with camping, hiking, and

Cut moss agate from Hachita.

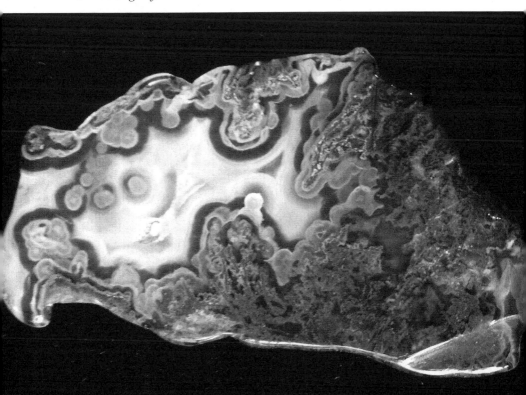

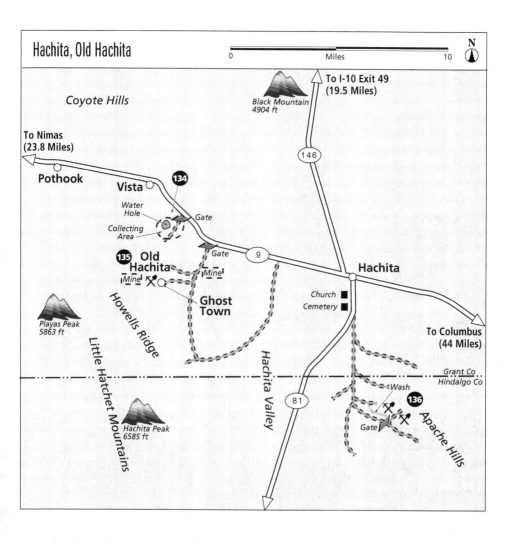

N

0   Miles   10

Coyote Hills

Black Mountain
4904 ft

**To I-10 Exit 49
(19.5 Miles)**

**To Nimas
(23.8 Miles)**

146

Pothook

Vista

134

Water
Hole

Gate

Collecting
Area

135 **Old
Hachita**

Gate

9

Hachita

Mine

Mine

**Ghost
Town**

Church
Cemetery

Howells Ridge

*Playas Peak
5863 ft*

**To Columbus
(44 Miles)**

Little Hatchet Mountains

Grant Co
Hindalgo Co

Wash

Hachita Valley

81

136

*Hachita Peak
6585 ft*

Gate

Apache Hills

wildlife watching. Quaint and artsy shops can be found in the towns of Rodeo, New Mexico, and Portal, Arizona. Shakespeare Ghost Town, just outside of Lordsburg, is a theme park built around the old mining town of Shakespeare. The Rockhound Roundup, one of the premier gem and mineral shows in the Southwest, usually takes place during the first couple weeks of March. The show is put on by the Deming Gem and Mineral Society (see appendix D) at the Southwest New Mexico State Fairgrounds in Deming.

Finding the site: From the junction of Highways 338 and 9 in Animas, turn left (east) onto Highway 9 and drive 23.8 miles to an unmarked dirt road on the right (south). Open the gate (be sure to close it behind you) and drive 0.4 mile to a parking area near a water hole. From Hachita, go 6.2 miles west on Highway 9 to the dirt road.

Rockhounding

You can find some very pretty agate in this area. Most of the pieces are small and suitable for tumbling, but some are large enough to slice. The larger pieces take a bit of time to find, but they are there. The agate has moss inclusions that run from red and black to green. The black variety looks very much like the famous Montana agate from the Yellowstone River. The real prize, and we found only one piece, is agate with drops of red included in the matrix, which closely resembles Utah's pigeon blood agate. We also found one nice-size piece of a pink banded agate that wound up making three beautiful cabs.

This site is must for any agate lover. Simply walk around and inspect any suspect piece. You may want to crack a few to see what is inside before dragging them home. We also found jasper in a mixture of red and green, as well as nicely patterned rhyolite.

If you do not want to drive onto the dirt road, some material can be found in the right-of-way of Highway 9 outside the gate.

Old Hachita Mine

See map on page 218.
Land type: Desert and mountain foothills.
GPS: N31° 54' 51" / W108° 25' 40".
Elevation: 4,803 feet.
Best time of year: October through May.
Land manager: Bureau of Land Management, Las Cruces District.
Material: Chrysacolla, chalcopyrite, calcite, garnet, azurite, bornite, malachite, galena, sphalerite, stibnite, chalcocite, and wolframite.
Tools: Geological hammer and spray bottle.
Vehicle: High-clearance four-wheel drive.
Precautions and restrictions: This is a very remote site, so be sure that your vehicle is in good shape and you have enough fuel and water. It can get very hot here in summer, and we were told that snakes are common during the warm months. Look out for open abandoned mining pits in the area.
Special attractions: Chiricahua National Monument boasts some of the most unusual rock formations in North America, along with camping, hiking, and wildlife watching. Quaint and artsy shops can be found in the towns of Rodeo, New Mexico, and Portal, Arizona. Shakespeare Ghost Town, just outside of Lordsburg, is a theme park built around the old mining town of Shakespeare. The Rockhound Roundup, one of the premier gem and mineral shows in the Southwest, usually takes place during the first couple weeks of March. The show is put on by the Deming Gem and Mineral Society (see appendix D) at the Southwest New Mexico State Fairgrounds in Deming.
Finding the site: From Hachita, drive 4.7 miles west on Highway 9 to a gravel road on the left (south). Turn left, pass through the gate (be sure to close it behind you), and go 1.7 miles to a fork. Take the right (southwest) fork and drive 0.6 mile to the old town site.

Rockhounding

Though extensive dumps can be found here, there appears to be very little collectible material. We found a bit of chrysacolla, a few rocks with garnet in them, some desert glass, and a couple small azurite crystals, and others have reported azurite, bornite, malachite, galena, sphalerite, stibnite, chalcocite, and wolframite.

Though the rockhounding here is rather poor, the trip is worthwhile to investigate the old ghost town.

Apache Mining District– Apache Mine #2

See map on page 218.
Land type: Desert.
GPS: N31° 50' 39" / W108° 18' 21".
Elevation: 4,709 feet.
Best time of year: October through May.
Land manager: Bureau of Land Management, Las Cruces District.
Material: Malachite, azurite, chrysocolla, calcite, hematite, chalcopyrite, cerussite, magnetite, hematite, quartz, bornite, and scheelite.
Tools: Geological hammer and spray bottle.
Vehicle: High-clearance four-wheel drive.
Precautions and restrictions: This is a very remote site, so be sure that your vehicle is in good shape and you have enough fuel and water. It can get very hot here in summer, and we were told that snakes are very common during the warm months. Look out for open abandoned mining pits in the area.
Special attractions: This site is near the New Mexico Birding Highway. Chiricahua National Monument boasts some of the most unusual rock formations in North America, along with camping, hiking, and wildlife watching. Shakespeare Ghost Town, just outside of Lordsburg, is a theme park built around the old mining town of Shakespeare. The Rockhound Roundup, one of the premier gem and mineral shows in the Southwest, usually takes place during the first couple weeks of March. The show is put on by the Deming Gem and Mineral Society (see appendix D) at the Southwest New Mexico State Fairgrounds in Deming.
Finding the site: From Hachita, drive south on Highway 81 for 1.3 miles to an unmarked rough road that intersects the highway at about 45 degrees on the left (east) side. Turn onto this road, which heads almost due south. After 0.9 mile you will pass a road coming in from the left (east), and in another mile another road will come in from the left. Continue straight for 0.6 mile and pass a road that joins on the right (west), then go another 0.5 mile to where a road from the east comes in. Continue straight again for another 0.2 mile and pass a road off on the right, then go straight ahead for 0.9 mile and turn left (southeast). You'll come to a gate and see a large wash on the left. Park here.

Rockhounding

We found malachite, azurite, chrysocolla, calcite, hematite, chalcopyrite, cerussite, magnatite, hematite, and quartz at this mine. Others have bornite and scheelite. Visitors to the site will start seeing pieces with the telltale green and blue of copper ore before reaching the gate. The dumps are extensive and would take many days to explore.

There may be claim issues here. The posted signs were very old and we could not determine whether they were valid at the time of our visit. Some folks in Hachita were skeptical, but it would probably be a good idea to check with the Grant County Clerk and the Hildalgo County Clerk (see appendix B).

Victorio Mining District

Land type: High desert.

GPS: N32° 10' 47" / W108° 05' 27".

Elevation: 4,482 feet.

Best time of year: October through May.

Land manager: Bureau of Land Management, Las Cruces District.

Material: Barite, barite crystals, quartz crystals, druzy quartz, malachite, chrysocolla, hematite, calcite, an unidentified white botroydal mineral, wulfenite, azurite, pyrite, galena, helvite, chalcocite, and cerussite.

Tools: Geological hammer.

Vehicle: Any vehicle will do until the last mile, at which point four-wheel drive is recommended.

Precautions and restrictions: Mine tailings can be slippery and treacherous, particularly those that are high and steep. Wear sturdy shoes. Always be on the lookout for mine shafts or deep holes, and never enter a mining shaft or tunnel.

Special attractions: Chiricahua National Monument boasts some of the most unusual rock formations in North America, along with camping, hiking, and wildlife watching. Shakespeare Ghost Town, just outside of Lordsburg, is a theme park built around the old mining town of Shakespeare. The Rockhound Roundup, one of the premier gem and mineral shows in the Southwest, usually takes place during the first couple weeks of March. The show is put on by the Deming Gem and Mineral Society (see appendix D) at the Southwest New Mexico State Fairgrounds in Deming.

Finding the site: There are numerous mines in the Victorio Mountains west of Deming that once produced gold, lead, silver, and zinc ores. From Deming, take Interstate 10 west about 18 miles to exit 62 (Gage). Head south 2.2 miles on an unmarked paved road, then bear southwest on a gravel road. After passing a large quarry on the left, a four-wheel-drive vehicle is recommended. At 1.1 miles you will see mine tailings and diggings on the hillside on the left. Park and walk uphill to the mines.

Rockhounding

Extensive mine dumps dot the hills in this region. We explored only a small area and found a variety of mineral specimens: barite, barite crystals, quartz crystals, druzy quartz, malachite, chrysocolla, hematite, calcite, and an unidentified white botroydal mineral. Others have reported wulfenite, azurite, pyrite, galena, helvite, chalcocite, and cerussite.

Deming Mines

Land type: Desert.

Best time of year: Usually during the first couple weeks of March, when tours are given (see below).

Land manager: Deming Gem and Mineral Society.

Material: Agates, agate nodules, and crystals.

Tools: Shovels and picks.

Vehicle: Any.

Special attractions: Chiricahua National Monument boasts some of the most unusual rock formations in North America, along with camping, hiking, and wildlife watching. Shakespeare Ghost Town, just outside of Lordsburg, is a theme park built around the old mining town of Shakespeare.

Precautions and restrictions: Collecting allowed only during tours.

Finding the site: The mines are located south of Deming. Tours are only available through the Deming Gem and Mineral Society.

A big boulder of picture rock at the Deming site.

Rockhounding

We have never been to this location; unfortunately, our timing was never quite right. The information we provide has been gathered from other sources.

The Deming area has been famous for beautiful agates and geodes for a long time. The primary claim, the Big Diggings, is now controlled by the Deming Gem and Mineral Society. This claim has some of the nicest agate found in North America. The colors run from red to vivid yellow to blue to black, and the patterns include moss, fortification, lace, and swirled mosaics.

Tours to this area only take place during the club's show, the Rockhound Roundup, which is usually held during the first couple weeks in March. Participants are charged a modest fee, which is a small price to pay for what can be picked up. For more information on these trips, contact the Deming Gem and Mineral Society (see appendix D).

Rockhound State Park

Land type: Rocky high desert.
Best time of year: October through May.
Land manager: New Mexico State Parks.
Material: Agate, jasper, and geodes.
Tools: Geological hammer, large pick, sledgehammer, various shovels, chisels, gads, crowbar, and goggles; masks if you have a problem with dust.
Vehicle: Any.
Precautions and restrictions: This is hard work and though the hike is short, it's relatively steep. Know your limits. It can be very hot here in summer, and there are snakes and other poisonous things around during warm months.
Special attractions: Chiricahua National Monument boasts some of the most unusual rock formations in North America, along with camping, hiking, and wildlife watching. Shakespeare Ghost Town, just outside of Lordsburg, is a theme park built around the old mining town of Shakespeare. The Rockhound Roundup, one of the premier gem and mineral shows in 0the Southwest, usually takes place during the first couple weeks of March. The show is put on by the Deming Gem and Mineral Society (see appendix D) at the Southwest New Mexico State Fairgrounds in Deming.
Finding the site: From the junction of Highways 549 and 11 in Deming, drive 6 miles west on Highway 549 to Highway 143. Turn right (south) onto Highway 143 and after 5.9 miles turn right (southeast) again onto Highway 198. Proceed to the park entrance on the left (east).

Rockhounding

The state of New Mexico set this site aside as a park especially for rockhounds. The primary target of most are the geodes that are embedded in the hillside. It's a pretty good walk up to the diggings, and the geodes are difficult to remove. It takes a lot of hard rock mining, but the rewards are well worth the effort. The interiors are beautiful. Many have hollow centers with quartz and/or calcite or other species of crystals surrounded by agate. Even the solid nodules have beautiful agate interiors. These geodes and nodules are not usually very colorful, but the black, white, clear, and shades of gray patterns are very beautiful.

Kilbourne Hole

Land type: Desert.
GPS: N31° 57' 25" / W106° 57' 30".
Elevation: 1,292 feet.
Best time of year: November through April.
Material: Peridot and jasper.
Land manager: Bureau of Land Management, Las Cruces District.
Tools: Geological hammer.
Vehicle: Four-wheel drive.
Precautions and restrictions: This is a very remote area, so make sure that your vehicle is in good shape and you have enough fuel and water. The Border Patrol is usually working in the area, and a lot of locals hunt for rabbits and target shoot here. Be careful of snakes and other poisonous critters.
Finding the site: Kilbourne Hole is located southwest of Las Cruces and northwest of El Paso, Texas. From exit 11 on Interstate 10, head west on Highway 184 (Country Club Road) for 2.6 miles. Turn right (north) onto Highway 273 and drive 1.7 miles to a left (west) onto Airport Road. Go 2.5 miles and pass the intersection with Highway 136. Continue 0.4 mile and cross railroad tracks. Turn right (northwest) onto an unmarked gravel road paralleling the railroad tracks and drive 1.4 miles. You will cross a cattle guard and then in another 4.8 miles, a second cattle guard. Go straight for another 4.3 miles, where yet another cattle guard will be crossed. After another 0.4 mile make a left (west) onto County Road A011. After 4.1 miles you will cross a desert road. Continue another 3.9 miles, passing a green water tank on the left (north) side, to Kilbourne Hole.

Rockhounding

This site boasts some very gemmy peridot. The stones were formed when a volcano erupted about 80,000 years ago. They come in the form of "bombs," which are plain brown on the outside. When chopped open, the clear green gems are obvious.

When you get to the crater, climb up the rim and then down into the hole. The bombs are rather difficult to spot, as they look like most of the other rocks. Once you figure it out, though, they will become apparent.

Kilbourne Hole

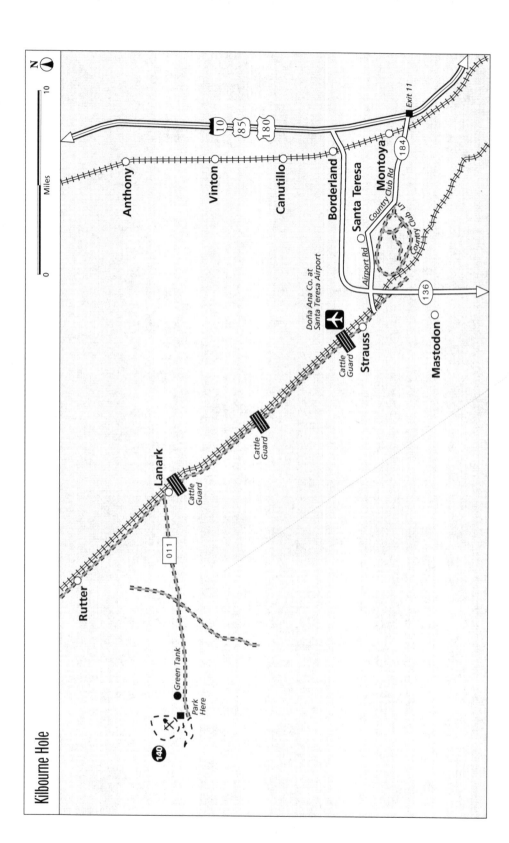

Most of the peridot grains inside the bombs are too small to do much with. We mixed a bunch of them with epoxy and then polished the conglomerate like a cab. The result was quite pretty. Some of the bombs hold coarse grains, and it's possible to find pieces that could be faceted into ¼- to ½-carat gems, though these are very scarce.

Who knows? You may find the bomb that has 1- or 2-carat stones inside. Good luck!

Appendix A: Glossary

Agate: A form of chalcedony containing bands or mossy inclusions; often very colorful, but sometimes with either one color or very muted colors.

Aggregate: A mixture of different kinds of rocks or crystals.

Alabaster: A fine-grained variety of gypsum used widely for carving.

Amethyst: A gemstone of the quartz family, ranging in color from pale lilac to deep purple.

Ammonite: A cephalopod fossil curled like a ram's horn.

Apache tears: a kind of nodular obsidian (volcanic black glass). When polished, it is opaque to nearly translucent. The color ranges from red to brown to black.

Aquamarine: A form of beryl next in desirability to emerald; colors range from pale to deep blue or blue green.

Aragonite: A form of calcite that often forms in layers or bands and is sometimes mistaken for onyx.

Azurite: A blue copper carbonate often associated with malachite.

Baculite: A cephalopod fossil of the same family as the ammonite, but straight rather than curled.

Barite: Barium sulfate occurring in blue, green, brown, and red colors.

Beryl: Beryllium aluminum sulphate that is colorless in its pure form; varieties include emerald, green; aquamarine, blue; morganite, pink; and heliodor, brown to golden yellow.

Biotite: A member of the mica group usually in black, brown black, or green black.

Book: Term for a common occurrence of mica in leaves that resemble the pages of a book.

Brachiopod: A marine animal with two nearly symmetrical shells, but with one slightly larger than the other.

Cabbing: The act of creating a cabochon.

Cabochon (Cab): A common shape for a gem, usually with an elliptical perimeter and a domed top.

Calcite: Calcium carbonate that occurs in clear as well as white, brown, red, yellow, and blue crystals.

Candy rock: See *picture rock.*

Cephalopod: Free-swimming marine animal; ammonites and baculites are typical of cephalopods.

Chalcedony: A cryptocrystalline form of quartz in which the crystal structure is not visible to the naked eye; forms include agate, jasper, carnelian, sard, onyx, chrysoprase, sardonyx, rose, and flint.

Cleavelandite: A form of albite in the plagioclase feldspar group.

Concretion: A cemented accumulation of mineral material; may contain pyrite, silica, calcite, or gypsum.

Country rock: The common rock surrounding a vein or other deposit of gemstones or minerals.

Crinoid: One of hundreds of round stem-like echinoderms; usually only parts are found as fossils.

Crystal: A solid mineral having a regular geometric shape with flat faces or surfaces.

Dendrite: A mineral inclusion in a rock which resembles the branching of a fern.

Dike: A wall of igneous rock surrounded by country rock.

Epidote: Green crystal sometimes used as a gemstone, but more commonly collected for display.

Feldspar: The most abundant mineral in the Earth's crust; classified as orthoclase and plagioclase; among the most desired varieties are moonstone, sunstone, microcline, and labradorite.

Float: Gemstones or minerals that have been transported from their place of origin by water, erosion, or gravity.

Fluorite: A common mineral that occurs in colors of white, brown, purple, green, yellow, violet, and blue; sometimes faceted, but too soft to stand up to day-to-day wear as jewelry.

Fluorspar: A less pure and more granular form of fluorite.

Fortification agate: Agate with acutely banded corners that form a closed figure resembling a fort.

Fossils: Remains of plants, insects, or animals preserved in casts or molds.

Gad: A chisel or pointed iron or steel bar used for loosening ore or rock.

Gangue: Country rock, or other rock of no value, surrounding minerals or gemstones.

Garnet: A group of differently colored but chemically similar minerals; group includes pyrope, red with brown; almandine, red with violet; spessartite, orange to red brown; grossular, yellow to copper brown; demantoid, emerald green; and uvarovite, emerald green.

Gem: A gemstone that has been prepared for use in jewelry.

Gemstone: Any precious or semiprecious stone that can be cut and/or polished and used in jewelry.

Geode: A hollow nodule or concretion, usually filled with crystal formations.

Gypsum: A hydrous calcium sulphate that occurs in white, colorless, gray, brown, red, and yellow; colorless variety is called selenite, and dense form is called alabaster.

Igneous: Rock formed by solidification or crystallization of magma; one of the three primary classifications of rock.

Jasper: Opaque form of chalcedony, often with mossy inclusions or intertwining of various colors.

Lapidary: The art of forming and shaping gemstones; one who forms or shapes gemstones.

Lepidolite: Pink to lilac-colored silicate mineral of the mica group.

Limonite: A term applied generally to a brownish iron hydroxide; often occurs as a pseudomorph after iron minerals such as pyrite.

Malachite: A green copper ore that occurs both in crystal and massive forms; massive forms are often banded, and many contain beautiful bull's-eyes.

Massive form: The form of a mineral in which the crystals are either very small or without any discernible definition.

Matrix: Material in which a mineral crystal or fossil is embedded.

Metamorphic: Pre-existing rock changed by the action of pressure, chemical action, or heat; one of the three primary classifications of rock.

Mica: A group of sheet silicate minerals, major members of which are muscovite, biotite, phlogopite, lepidolite, and chlorite.

Micromount: A tiny mineral specimen intended for viewing under a microscope.

Muscovite: One of the mica group; usually colorless to pale yellow, green, pink, or brown.

Onyx: A black- and white-banded chalcedony; colored varieties sold in gift shops are either dyed onyx or a form of calcite or aragonite.

Opal: A silicon oxide closely related to chalcedony, but softer and containing water. Common opal is often dull and not suitable for jewelry, but some has a waxy texture and will cut and polish into nice cabochons; often replaces wood fibers in fossil wood and makes finely detailed samples. Precious opal is the type associated with fine jewelry and shows beautiful flashes of multicolored fire; often mistakenly called fire opal, but true fire opal is red and does not have the flashes of fire.

Pegmatite: Coarse-grained igneous rock often the host for gemstones and minerals; usually found as smaller masses in large igneous formations.

Pelecypods: Bivalved mollusks with shells that meet evenly at the hinge; not symmetrical as in the brachiopods; oysters, clams, and mussels are typical pelecypods.

Petrification: The process by which silica or other minerals replace the cell structure of organic material.

Picture rock: A swirly patterned rhyolite used for jewelry and decorative pieces. Also called *candy rock*.

Porphyry: Rock containing crystals in a fine-grained mass.

Pseudomorph: A crystal with the geometric appearance of one mineral, but which has been chemically replaced with another mineral.

Pyrite: Iron sulfide or disulfide with a brassy yellow color; commonly called "fools' gold."

Quartz (Cryptocrystalline): Group that includes amethyst, aventurine, citrine, rose quartz, smoky quartz, and tiger eye.

Quartz (Macrocrystalline): Group that includes chalcedony, agate, jasper, onyx, chrysoprase, and sard.

Rhodochrosite: A manganese carbonate gemstone in colors from rose red to white with striping; sometimes forms as stalactites in caves.

Rhodonite: A deep red to pink gemstone usually with black manganese oxide inclusions that often appear as spider webbing.

Sedimentary: Rock formed by deposition, compaction, and cementation; one of the three primary classifications of rock.

Silicafied: A mineral or organic compound that has been replaced by silica.

Tailings: Waste material from mining or milling.

Zeolite: Any of various hydrous silicates that are analogous in composition to the feldspars and occur as secondary minerals in cavities of lavas.

Appendix B: Land Managers and Government Offices

County Clerks

Bernalillo County Clerk
One Civic Plaza NW, Sixth Floor
Albuquerque, NM 87102
(505) 468-1290
clerk@bernco.gov

Catron County Clerk
P.O. Box 507
Reserve, NM 87830
(505) 533-6400
cclerk2@gilanet.com

Chavez County Clerk
#1 St. Mary's Place, Suite 110
Roswell, NM 88203
(505) 624-6614
coclerk@co.chaves.nm.us

Colfax County Clerk
County Courthouse
230 North Third Street
P.O. Box 159
Raton, NM 87740
(505) 445-5551

Curry County Clerk's Office
700 North Main Street, Suite 7
P.O. Box 1168
Clovis, NM 88101
(505) 763-5591
mtrujillo@currycounty.org

Eddy County Clerk
Eddy County Administration
 Complex
101 West Greene Street
Carlsbad, NM 88220-6219
(505) 885-3383

Grant County Clerk Directory
Grant County Administration
 Building
1400 Highway 180 East
Silver City, NM 88061
(505) 574-0000

Harding County Clerk
35 Pine Street
P.O. Box 1002
Mosquero, NM 87733
(505) 673-2301
hardingcc@plateautel.net

Lea County Clerk
P.O. Box 1507
Lovington, NM 88260
(505) 396-8614
mhughes@leacounty.net

Lincoln County Clerk
P.O. Box 338
Carrizozo, NM 88301-0338
(505) 648-2394, ext. 131, or (800)
687-2705
tammiemaddox@lincolncounty
 nm.net

Los Alamos County Clerk
Los Alamos County Municipal
  Building
2300 Trinity Drive, Room 100
(505) 662-8010
clerks@mail.lacnm.us

Luna County Clerk's Office
321 West Spruce
P.O. Drawer 511
Deming, NM 88031
(505) 546-0491

Mckinley County Administration
207 West Hill Avenue
Gallup, NM 87301
(505) 722-3868

Quay County Government
300 South Third Street–Courthouse
P.O. Box 1246
Tucumcari, NM 88401
(505) 461-2112

Rio Arriba County Clerk
Espanola Office
Rio Arriba County Complex
1122 Industrial Park Road
Espanola, NM 87532
(505) 753-1780

Rio Arriba County Clerk
Tierra Amarilla Office
Tierra Amarilla Court House
P.O. Box 158
Tierra Amarilla, NM 87575
(505) 588-7724

Roosevelt County Clerk
County Courthouse, Room 106
Portales, NM 88130
(505) 356-8562

San Juan County Offices
100 South Oliver Drive
Aztec, NM 87410
(505) 334-9481

San Miguel County Administrative
  Aid
500 West National Avenue, Suite 100
Las Vegas, NM 87701
(505) 425-9333

Sierra County Clerk
300 Date Street
Truth or Consequences, NM
  87901-2362
(505) 894-2840
jsanchez@riolink.com

Taos County Clerk
105 Albright Street, Suite D
Taos, NM 87571
(505) 737-6380

Torrance County Clerk's Office
P.O. Box 767
Estancia, NM 87016
(505) 246-4735

Valencia County Clerk
444 Luna Avenue
P.O. Box 969
Los Lunas, NM 87031
(505) 866-2073
clk@co.valencia.nm.us

Bureau of Land Management (BLM) Offices

State Office
Bureau of Land Management
1474 Rodeo Road
Santa Fe, NM 87505
(505) 438-7400
Mailing address:
P.O. Box 27115
Santa Fe, NM 87502-0115

District Offices
Albuquerque District Office
435 Montano Road NE
Albuquerque, NM 87107
(505) 761-8700

Farmington District Office
1235 La Plata Highway, Suite A
Farmington, NM 87401-8731
(505) 599-8900

Las Cruces District Office
1800 Marquess Street
Las Cruces, NM 88005-3371
(505) 525-4300

Pecos District Office
2909 West Second Street
Roswell, NM 88201-2019
(505) 627-0272

Field Offices and Stations
Carlsbad Field Office
620 East Greene Street
Carlsbad, NM 88220-6292
(505) 887-6544

Cuba Field Station
County Road 11, Suite C
P.O. Box 670
Cuba, NM 87013
(505) 289-3748

Farmington Field Office
1235 La Plata Highway, Suite A
Farmington, NM 87401-8731
(505) 599-8900

Grants Field Station
P.O. Box 846
Grants, NM 87020
(505) 287-7911

Hobbs Field Station
414 West Taylor
Hobbs, NM 88240-1157
(505) 393-3612

Rio Puerco Field Office
435 Montano Road NE
Albuquerque, NM 87107-4935
(505) 761-8700

Roswell Field Office
2909 West Second Street
Roswell, NM 88201-2019
(505) 627-0272

Socorro Field Office
901 South Highway 85
Socorro, NM 87801-4168
(505) 835-0412

Taos Field Office
226 Cruz Alta Road
Taos, NM 87571-5983
(505) 758-8851

USDA Forest Service Offices

National Office
USDA Forest Service
1400 Independence Avenue SW
Washington, DC 20250-0003
(202) 205-8333

Southwestern Regional Office
USDA Forest Service
333 Broadway SE
Albuquerque, NM 87102
(505) 842-3292

Carson National Forest
Carson National Forest Main Office
208 Cruz Alta Road
Taos, NM 87571
(505) 758-6200

Camino Real Ranger District
P.O. Box 68
Penasco, NM 87553
(505) 587-2255

Canjilon Ranger District
P.O. Box 469
Canjilon, NM 87515
(505) 684-2489

El Rito Ranger District
P.O. Box 56
El Rito, NM 87530
(505) 581-4554

Jicarilla Ranger District
664 East Broadway
Bloomfield, NM 87413
(505) 632-2956

Questa Ranger District
P.O. Box 110
Questa, NM 87556
(505) 586-0520

Tres Piedras Ranger District
P.O. Box 38
Tres Piedras, NM 87577
(505) 758-8678

Cibola National Forest
Cibola National Forest Main Office
2113 Osuna Road NE, Suite A
Albuquerque, NM 87113
(505) 346-3900

Kiowa and Rita Blanca National
  Grassland
714 Main Street
Clayton, NM 88415
(505) 374-9652

Magdalena Ranger District
P.O. Box 45
Magdalena, NM 87825-0001
(505) 854-2281

Mount Taylor Ranger District
1800 Lobo Canyon Road
Grants, NM 87020
(505) 287-8833

Mountainair Ranger District
1800 Lobo Canyon Road
Grants, NM 87020
(505) 287-8833

Sandia Ranger District
11776 Highway 337
Tijeras, NM 87059-8619
(505) 281-3304

Gila National Forest

Gila National Forest Main Office
3005 East Camino del Bosque
Silver City NM 88061
(505) 388-8201

Black Range Ranger District
1804 North Date Street
Truth or Consequences, NM 87901
(505) 894-6677

Glenwood Ranger District
P.O. Box 8
Glenwood, NM 88039
(505) 539-2481

Quemado Ranger District
P.O. Box 159
Quemado, NM 87829
(505) 773-4678

Reserve Ranger District
P.O. Box 170
Reserve, NM 87830
(505) 533-6232

Silver City Ranger District
3005 East Camino del Bosque
Silver City, NM 88061
(505) 388-8201

Wilderness Ranger District
HC 68, Box 50
Mimbres, NM 88049
(505) 536-2250

Lincoln National Forest

Lincoln National Forest Main Office
1101 New York Avenue
Alamogordo, NM 88310
(505) 434-7200

Guadalupe Ranger District
Federal Building, Room 159
Carlsbad, NM 88220
(505) 885-4181

Sacramento Ranger District
P.O. Box 288
Cloudcroft, NM 88317
(505) 682-2551

Smokey Bear Ranger District
901 Mechem Drive
Ruidoso, NM 88345
(505) 257-4095

Santa Fe National Forest

Santa Fe National Forest Main
Office
1474 Rodeo Road
Santa Fe, NM 87505
(505) 438-7840

Coyote Ranger District
HC 78, Box 1
Coyote, NM 87012
(505) 638-5526

Cuba Ranger District
P.O. Box 130
Cuba, NM 87013
(505) 289-3264

Espanola Ranger District
1710 North Riverside Drive
P.O. Box 3307
Espanola, NM 87532
(505) 753-7331

Jemez Ranger District
P.O. Box 150
Jemez Springs, NM 87025
(505) 829-3535

Las Vegas Ranger Station
1926 North Seventh Street
Las Vegas, NM 87701
(505) 425-3534

Los Alamos Satellite Office
475 20th Street
Los Alamos, NM 87544
(505) 667-5120

Pecos/Las Vegas Ranger District
P.O. Drawer 429
Pecos, NM 87552
(505) 757-6121

Walatowa Visitor Center
7413 Highway 4
Pueblo of Jemez, NM 87024
(505) 834-7235

Carlsbad Caverns National Park
3225 National Parks Highway
Carlsbad, New Mexico 88220
(505) 785-2232 (visitor information)
(505) 785-3012 (bat flight
    information)
www.nps.gov/cave/contacts.htm

Clayton Lake State Park
141 Clayton Lake Road
Clayton, NM 88415
(505) 374-8808
www.emnrd.state.nm.us/prd/
    clayton.htm

New Mexico State Forestry Division
1220 South St. Francis Drive
P.O. Box 1948
Santa Fe, NM 87504-1948
(505) 476-3325

New Mexico State Land Office
310 Old Santa Fe Trail
Santa Fe, NM 87501
(505) 827-5760
Mailing address:
P.O. Box 1148
Santa Fe, NM 87504-1148

Other Useful Contacts

Capulin Volcano National Monument
P.O. Box 40
Capulin, NM 88414
(505) 278-2201
www.nps.gov/cavo/contacts.htm

Appendix C: Special Attractions

A. R. Mitchell Memorial Museum
and Gallery
150 East Main Street
Trinidad, CO 81082
(719) 846-4224
http://historictrinidad.com/tour/
mitch.html

Bandelier National Monument
15 Entrance Road
Los Alamos, NM 87544
(505) 672-3861, ext. 517
www.nps.gov/band

Bosque del Apache National Wildlife
Refuge Visitor Center
P.O. Box 1246
Socorro, NM 87801
(505) 835-1828
www.fws.gov/southwest/refuges/
newmex/bosque

Bottomless Lakes State Park
HC 12, Box 120
Roswell, NM 88201
(505) 624-6058
www.emnrd.state.nm.us/prd/
bottomless.htm

Box Car Museum
Main Street
Magdalena, NM 87119
(505) 854-2261

Branigan Cultural Center
501 North Main Street
Las Cruces, NM 88001
(505) 541-2155
www.las-cruces.org/public-services/
museums//branigan.shtm

Caballo Lake State Park
P.O. Box 32
Caballo, NM 87931
(505) 743-3942
www.emnrd.state.nm.us/prd/
caballo.htm

Catwalk National Recreation Trail
P.O. Box 8
Glenwood, NM 88039
(505) 539-2481
www2.srs.fs.fed.us/r3/gila/
recreation/attractions.asp?attid=1

Chaco Culture National
Historical Park
P. O. Box 220
Nageezi, NM 87037
(505) 786-7014
www.newmexico.org/place/loc/
parks/page/DB-place/place/352
.html

Chiricahua National Monument
12856 East Rhyolite Creek Road
Willcox, AZ 85643
(520) 824-3560
www.nps.gov/chir/contacts.htm

Cimarron Canyon State Park
P.O. Box 185
Eagle Nest, NM 87718
(575) 377-6271
www.emnrd.state.nm.us/prd/
cimarroncanyon.htm

Coyote Creek State Park
P.O. Box 477
Guadalupita, NM 87722
(505) 387-2328
www.emnrd.state.nm.us/prd/coyote
creek.htm

Dexter National Fish Hatchery
P.O. Box 219
Dexter, NM 88230
(505) 734-5910
www.fws.gov/southwest/fishery/
dexter.html

E. I. Couse Historic Home and Studio
146 East Kit Carson Road
Taos, NM 87571
(505) 751-0369
www.collectorsguide.com/ts/tsfa13
.shtml

El Camino Real International
    Heritage Center
County Road 1598
P.O. Box 175
Socorro, NM 87801
(505) 854-3600
www.caminorealheritage.org

Fort Sumner Chamber of Commerce
707 North Fourth Street
P.O. Box 28
Fort Sumner, NM 88119
www.ftsumnerchamber.com
(505) 355-7705
Fort Sumner attractions:
Old Fort Sumner Museum
(505) 355-2942
Fort Sumner State Monument
(505) 355-2573

Fort Union National Monument
P.O. Box 127
Watrous, NM 87753
(505) 425-8025
www.nps.gov/foun/contacts.htm

Gila Cliff Dwellings National
    Monument
HC 68, Box 100
Silver City, NM 88061
(575) 536-9461
www.nps.gov/gicl/

Gila Hot Springs Pools and
Campground
Highway 11, Box 80
Silver City, NM 88061
(575) 536-9314 (days)
(575) 536-9551 (evenings)

Guadalupe Mountains National Park
400 Pine Canyon Road
Salt Flat, TX 79847-9400
(915) 828-3251 (headquarters visitor
    center)
(505) 981-2418 (Dog Canyon
    Ranger Station)

Institute of American Indian Arts
83 Avan Nu Po Road
Santa Fe, NM 87508-1300
(505) 424-2300
www.iaia.edu

International UFO Museum &
　Research Center
114 North Main Street
Roswell, NM 88203
(800) 822-3545
www.roswellufomuseum.com

Jemez Springs Municipality
P.O. Box 269
Jemez Springs, NM 87025
(505) 829-3540
vclerk@jemezsprings.org

Las Cruces Museum of Natural
　History
700 South Telshor Boulevard
Las Cruces, NM 88011
(505) 522-3120
www.las-cruces.org/public-services/
　museums//nhm.shtm

Living Desert State Park
1500 Mills Drive
Carlsbad, NM 88220-3057
(505) 887-5516

Maxwell Museum of Anthropology
MSC01 1050
1 University of New Mexico
Albuquerque, NM 87131-0001
(505) 277-4405
www.unm.edu/~maxwell

Millicent Rogers Museum
1504 Museum Road
Taos, NM 87571
(505) 758-2462
www.millicentrogers.org

Mineral Museum of the New
　Mexico Bureau of Mines and
　Mineral Resources
New Mexico Institute of Mining
　and Technology
801 Leroy Place
Socorro, NM 87801
(505) 835-5420
www.geoinfo.nmt.edu

The Museum of Archeological and
　Material Culture
22 Calvary Road
Cedar Crest, NM 87008
(505) 281-2005
www.museumarch.org

Museum of International Folk Art
706 Camino Lejo
P.O. Box 2087
Santa Fe, NM 87504-2087
(505) 476-1200
www.moifa.org

National Radio Astronomy
　Observatory
Array Operations Center
1003 Lopezville Road
P.O. Box O
Socorro, NM 87801-0387
(505) 835-7000

New Mexico Museum of Natural
   History and Science
1801 Mountain Road NW
Albuquerque, NM 87104
(505) 841-2800
www.nmnaturalhistory.org

Ojo Caliente Mineral Springs Resort
50 Los Banos Road
P.O. Box 68
Ojo Caliente, NM 87549
(505) 583-2233
http://ojocalientesprings.com

Rio Grande Gorge Visitor Center
2873 North Highway 68
Pilar, NM 87571
(505) 751-4899

Rough Rider Memorial Collection
City of Las Vegas Museum
727 Grand Avenue
Las Vegas, NM 87701
(505) 454-1401, ext. 283
museum@desertgate.com

Royal Scepter Museum and
   Rock Shop
1805 Little Walnut Creek Road
Silver City, NM 88061
(877) 626-9001

Salinas Pueblo Missions National
   Monument
Corner of Ripley and Broadway
P.O. Box 517
Mountainair, NM 87036-0517
(505) 847-2585
www.nps.gov/sapu

City of Santa Rosa
141 South Fifth Street
Santa Rosa, NM 88435
(505) 472-3404
www.santarosanm.org

Shakespeare Ghost Town
P.O. Box 253
Lordsburg, NM 88045
(505) 542-9034
www.shakespeareghostown.com

Storrie Lake State Park
HC33, Box 109#2
Las Vegas, NM 87701
(505) 425-7278
www.emnrd.state.nm.us/prd/storrie
   lake.htm

Tinkertown Museum
121 Sandia Crest Drive
P.O. Box 303
Sandia Park, NM 87047
(505) 281-5233
www.tinkertown.com

Trinidad History Museum
300 East Main Street
Trinidad, CO 81082
(719) 846-7217
www.coloradohistory.org/hist_sites/
   trinidad/trinidad.htm

Turquoise Trail Association
P.O. Box 303
Sandia Park, NM 87047
www.turquoisetrail.org

Wildland Firefighters Museum
111 West Smokey Bear Boulevard
Capitan, NM 88316
www.southernnewmexico.com/
   Articles/Southeast/Lincoln/
   Capitan/WildlandFirefighter
   Museum.html
(505) 354-4251

Appendix D: New Mexico Gem and Mineral Societies

Though gem and mineral clubs come and go, here is a list of a few that were active when we wrote this book.

Albuquerque Gem & Mineral Club
P.O. Box 13718
Albuquerque, NM 87192-3718
(505) 345-0520 or (505) 889-9357

Chaparral Rockhounds
P.O. Box 815
Roswell, NM 88202
(505) 622-3144

Clovis Gem & Mineral Society
1587 Highway 60/84
Clovis, NM 88101
(806) 799-2224

Deming Gem and Mineral Society
P.O. Box 1459
Deming, NM 88031
(505) 267-4399, (505) 546-4338, or
   (505) 544-0838
http://dgms.bravehost.com

Grant County Rolling Stones Gem
& Mineral Society
P.O. Box 1555
Silver City, NM 88062-1555
(505) 388-9312 or (505) 534-9064

Lea Lap Rock & Mineral Club
P. O. Box 1065
Hobbs, NM 88241
(505) 392-2222

Los Alamos Geological Society
P.O. Box 762
Los Alamos, NM 87544-0762
http://home.netcome.com/
   ~hoffmans/LAGS.html

The New Mexico Faceters Guild
6800 Luella Anne NE
Albuquerque, NM 87109
www.attawaygems.com/NMFG

Rio Rancho Rockhounds
309 San Juan de Rio
Rio Rancho, NM 87124

Roadrunner Gem & Mineral Club
P.O. Box 1023
Carlsbad, NM 88220
(505) 885-1901 or (505) 887-0133

San Juan County Gem & Mineral
   Society
P.O. Box 1482
Farmington, NM 87499-1482
(505) 326-3567

Sierra Rock Club
206 Fur Street
Truth or Consequences, NM 87901

Appendix E: Additional Sites

In this appendix we list a number of sites that we have not yet visited or have not visited recently. The directions are crude and the information sketchy, but if you are in the area and looking for an adventure, why not try finding them? Some of these additional sites might also be under claim or otherwise in private hands. Always ask permission before rockhounding on private land.

Wind Mountain Minerals: This is a very remote location in the Cornudas Mountains, just north of the Texas state line. From U.S. Highway 54 south, turn left (east) onto Highway 506 and continue for 25 miles. Copper ores and other crystals can be found here.

Zuni Canyon Fluorite: Take Interstate 40 to exit 81 at Grants. Head south and cross the highway. You will soon see a sign to Highway 49. Drive about 10 miles to Forest Road 447 and turn left. Proceed 2.6 miles and turn right onto a dirt track. After 0.1 mile the track curves around to the right and another track enters from the left. Continue right for 2.8 miles, where you will see another track to the right. Take this new track and continue to the mine. The last time we were there, FR 447 was impassible. The directions are just approximate, but if you find the mine, you can pick up some beautiful fluorite.

Bear Springs Agate, Jasper, and Obsidian: This area is quite remote but supplies the rockhound with nice Apache tears, common opal, and agate. The region lies roughly between Cochiti Pueblo and Ponderosa. From Jemez Springs, drive south on Highway 4 to Highway 290 and turn left (west). Drive through Ponderosa and past Bear Springs, and start looking.

Jones Iron Mines: This remote area is a good source for magnetite and tabular crystals of hematite, and some micromounts of sphene, apatite, and actinolite are also found here. From U.S. Highway 380 near Bingham, take the Salinas National Monument–Gran Quivera Road north for about 8.5 miles. Turn east onto a small dirt road and continue another 6 miles to the mine dumps.

Nogal Mining Area: This old gold-mining area is located east of Carrizozo. Rockhounds may find gold, silver, lead, galena, and various species of pyrite. From Carrizozo, follow U.S. Highway 380 east to Highway 37, then turn south and drive 4 miles to Nogal. The mining area can be found by turning west on rough roads from the village.

Smokey Bear Quartz: This area has been closed because of abuse by rockhounds—apparently, a few collected here for commercial purposes. The Forest Service was not able to control the mining and decided to just close the area. This was a fantastic place to collect beautiful smokey quartz crystals and clusters. It's too bad that the actions of few resulted in the punishment of all, but it was a necessary step taken by the service. We include it in the event the location is reopened. Contact the Smokey Bear Ranger District of the Lincoln National Forest (see appendix B) for the current status.

Hansonburg Mining District: This is a "pay to collect" area. These mines are famous for fine specimens of blue fluorite, large galena cubes, blue linarite, and a variety of other minerals. The area is located a little south of Bingham off U.S. Highway 380. Contact the Blanchard Rock Shop, US 380, Bingham, NM 87815 (505-423-3235) for fee permits and directions to the mine.

Paramount Canyon Minerals: Located in the northwest corner of Sierra County, this area has produced nice specimens (mostly micromounts) of bixbyite, ilmenite, and beryl, among others. From the junction of Highways 52 and 59, follow Highway 59 about 20 miles west. The collecting area is to the south.

Iron Mountain Mine: Iron Mountain is located about 10 miles north of Winston. From Winston, take Highway 52 north for about 10 miles. Right before the junction of Highway 59, tracks heading toward the mountains will be seen on the right (east) side of the road. Park here and hike about 2 miles to the old mine. Thinking the road to this location was open, we traveled to the junction of Highways 52 and 59. The road off to the east was not there, even though it is shown on some maps. What we did find was tracks heading in the appropriate direction that were not drivable. We did not have the time to walk the short distance, but if you have the energy, this mine is probably worth the hike. Rockhounds can find copper and iron ores at this old mine.

Index

C

Caballo Lake State Park, 192, 193, 194

calcite: Northeastern, 57, 65, 79–82, 88; Northwestern, 30, 35–37, 48; Southeastern, 94, 98–99; Southwestern, 131–32, 137–39, 141–42, 151, 154, 158, 162, 168, 171, 175, 179, 183–85, 205–6, 212–114, 220–23

Camino Real, 130, 131, 133, 135, 137, 138, 140, 141, 144, 145

Capitan, 91, 94, 95, 98, 99, 100, 103, 104

Capulin Volcano National Monument, 61, 62, 63

Carlsbad and Carlsbad Caverns National Park, 107, 108, 109, 111, 112

carnelian: Northwestern, 15, 19, 52–54; Southeastern, 104; Southwestern, 127, 138–39, 152, 189, 207–9

Carrizozo, 97

Catwalk National Recreation Trail, 147, 148, 149, 151, 152, 153, 154, 156, 158, 159, 160, 162

Cedar Crest, 77, 79, 82

Cerrillos Hills Historic Park, 83

cerussite, 91–93, 133–34, 137, 221–23

chabazite, 171–72

Chaco Culture National Historical Park, 13, 15, 17, 44, 45

chalcedony, 49, 115–17, 156, 190, 194, 201–2

chalcedony roses: Northwestern, 39, 49; Southwestern, 141–43, 146, 158, 160, 163, 166, 173–74, 190, 195–98

chalcocite: Northwestern, 20; Southeastern, 91; Southwestern, 120, 124–26, 162, 179, 220, 223

chalcopyrite: Northeastern, 57, 71; Northwestern, 20; Southeastern, 91; Southwestern, 133–34, 138, 162, 179, 183–85, 212–13, 220–22

chatoyance, 46

Chavez Canyon, 141–43

chert, 44, 176

Chihuahuan Desert, 107, 108, 109, 112

Chiricahua National Monument, 212, 214, 215–16, 217–18, 220, 221, 223, 224, 226

chlorargyrite, 183–85

Chloride, 183–85

chrysacolla: Northwestern, 20; Southeastern, 91; Southwestern, 124, 179, 183–85, 205–6, 212–14, 220–23

chrysoprase, 131–32

Chupadera Mountains, 140

Cimarron Canyon State Park, 57, 58, 60

Cimarron Mesa, 123

City of Las Vegas Museum, 72, 76

Clayton Lake State Park, 61, 62, 64

cleavelandite, 65

Cloudcroft, 107, 108, 109

collection restrictions, 8–9

Contreras, 130

Cookes Peak, 207–9

Copperas Peak, 173–74

copper ore, 93, 139, 179, 212, 222

cougars, 5

Coyote, 23

Coyote Creek State Park, 57, 58, 60

volcanoes and lava flows:
    Northeastern, 63; Southeastern,
    97; Southwestern, 115, 118, 119,
    120, 122, 123

W

weather, 8
Whites City, 107, 108, 109, 112
wilderness areas, 9
Wildland Firefighters Museum, 91,
    94, 95, 98, 99, 100, 103, 104
wolframite, 220
wulfenite, 91–93, 133–34, 137, 223

Z

zeolites, 37, 48, 94, 99, 164–65,
    171–72
Zuni Nation, 120–21
Zuni Salt Lake, 115, 118, 119,
    120–22, 123

About the Authors

Ruta Vaskys and Martin Freed have had a number of careers, including faculty appointments at various colleges, entrepreneurs, trapping and collecting wild herbs in Vermont and Alaska, and outdoors and conservation writers and photographers. They've been prospecting all of North America for the past thirty years, and for the last fifteen years they've been collecting minerals and turning them into beautiful pieces of art.

Ruta has a BS in occupational therapy and a master's in counseling. She has worked in both fields and has been a professional commercial artist. She studied at the Maryland Institute of Art and the Richmond Professional Institute, and did her graduate studies at the University of Alaska, Fairbanks. Martin has taught geology, chemistry, oceanography, and mathematics at a number of

Martin Freed and Ruta Vaskys

colleges and universities. He graduated from Coastal Carolina with a BS and did his graduate work at the University of Alaska in physical oceanography.

Before going to graduate school, the couple built a cabin in the Green Mountains of Vermont and lived without electricity or running water for a number of years. After graduate school, Martin and Ruta made Alaska their home. In 1988 they bought another home on the Eastern Shore of Virginia and currently split the year between the two states, taking time in the winter to travel the Southwest pursuing their rockhounding passion.

Ruta and Martin started writing about the outdoors in the mid-1980s and have had articles published in many regional and national publications, including *Fur-Fish-Game, Easy Street,* the *Eastern Shore News,* the *Mid-Atlantic Fisherman, What's Up Annapolis, Shotgun Magazine, Chesapeake Angler Magazine, Maryland Life,* the *Salisbury Times, Alaska, Fly Fisherman, Fish Alaska,* and *Game & Fish.* Both are members of the Outdoor Writers Association of America (OWAA). The couple's first book, *Fishing Virginia,* was published in 2007, and *Fishing Maryland, Delaware, and Washington, D.C.* was published in 2008 (both by The Lyons Press).

Ruta and Martin met on top of Mount Abraham in Vermont in 1976 and have been climbing mountains together ever since.

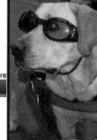